SALMON RIVER FIRE

Thirty Years

An Idaho Fire Fighter

John Sangster

Cover photos by David Rauzi /Idaho County Free Press

Copyright @ 2013 John Sangster

ALL RIGHTS RESERVED

SALMON RIVER FIRE:

Thirty Years An Idaho Firefighter

COPYRIGHT © 2013 John Sangster

ALL RIGHTS RESERVED

ISBN 10: 0-615-83026-9

ISBN 13: 978-0-615-83026-1

NO PART OF THIS BOOK MAY BE REPRODUCED OR TRANSMITTED IN ANY FORM OR ANY MANNER, ELECTRONIC OR MECHANICAL, INCLUDING PHOTOCOPYING, RECORDING OR BY ANY INFORMATION STORAGE AND RETRIEVAL SYSTEM, WITHOUT PERMISSION IN WRITING FROM THE AUTHOR.

PRIVACY NOTICE: Some – but not all – of the names and locations in this book have been changed in the interests of privacy. The stories, however, are all based on fact.

*For Mom, Dad, Cindy, Dominic
And Carmen*

PREFACE	v
A Young Boy and Fire	3
Hotshots	15
Interregional Fire Crew	49
The Salmon River, Part One	67
Mt. Hood	73
The Salmon River, Part Two	93
Double Duty Volunteer	119
The New Century	133
Blackerby	151
Seven Devils and Combines	159
Poe Cabin	165
Parsonage and Gas Station	177
Wind-Driven Field Fire	187
Hungry Flames	193
Barn and Vehicles	199
Long 2012 Season	205
Still Going	213

PREFACE

Fire. The clinical definition of fire, as per the National Fire Protection Association, is a chemical reaction of combining oxygen with a substance. This reaction happens extremely fast, producing light, heat, and noise. Break or prevent the chemical reaction and there is no fire.

For fire fighters, looking at fire as a chemical reaction is just not romantic. Hence, fire becomes an object, such as a dragon. Then we become soldiers or knights, working together to corral and then slay the wicked beast, the dragon called fire.

During the past 40 years of fighting fires throughout the Western United States, over 30 of these years in Idaho, I have had the privilege of working together with a bunch of great people. Jumping into battle against the evil beast brings out the best in many, the worst in a few. Needing to work together because lives depend on the teamwork leads to a strong and long lasting bond. This camaraderie is probably the greatest side benefit of the fire fighting effort.

For those of you that have fought fires, you have experienced this unique bond, the camaraderie that lasts for years. It doesn't matter whether you are a wildland fire fighter, a volunteer working in the wildland urban interface, or a paid fire fighter working in the busy city. Camaraderie is what gets us through the tough times.

There is a lot of pride in the successful protection of homes or the quick stop of a fire on the verge of growing big. There are also those times of pain when our best efforts were in vain, or if only, we could have arrived a few minutes earlier. It's a team effort so we share in the ups and downs.

Many of you will recognize and relate to some of the events portrayed in these stories. Others can rightly say *"you think you had it tough!"* These stories are told for two reasons: to tell what it's like to be a wildland and volunteer firefighter; and to remind those who came before me and those who are with me now that we are part of the history, the evolution forming the future firefighters.

As I was finishing this preface, I learned of the tragic loss of nineteen members of the Granite Mountain Hot Shots. In this book I mention some of the tragic fires that had occurred up to 1970, when I first started fighting fire. After 1970, some of the significant years of multiple tragedies include: 1994, South Canyon fire, 14 firefighters killed; 2001, Thirty Mile fire, 4 firefighters died while in their shelters; 2006, Esperanza fire, an engine crew of 5 killed by an intense area flash over. This list does not include the hundreds of firefighters, both wildland and urban firefighters, killed in less newsworthy but just as tragic fires. At some of the State wide fire meetings and training sessions, the opening ceremony includes the ringing of the bell, the tribute to those who paid the ultimate price for being a firefighter. We shall not forget.

Firefighting is dangerous-no doubt about it. But firefighting does have its good times too. As Ben Walters remarked in the Preface of his book *Fire Crew: Stories From The Fireline*, Ben Walters 2011, "It was fun, wasn't it?" Yes, many times the battle has been fun, until the fire has an appetite for homes, or much worse becomes a killer. But when we look back on a good stop or a good save, didn't it feel great?

Dennis Smith, in his ground breaking book *Report From Engine Company 82*, Warner Books 1972, writes in his introduction: "In the end, what is most admirable about firefighters is their reliability: when they are called, they come." This seems to say it all.

SALMON RIVER FIRE

It was a typical Sunday morning, at least for the first couple of hours. After feeding the dogs and cats, I patiently waited for the last perk of the coffeemaker. I sat down with a fresh cup in hand and checked the online news, then went into the kitchen and started breakfast for my wife, Cindy, and me. When I stepped outside to retrieve my thermos from the car, I happened to look south to the forested hills beyond the southern edge of the city of Grangeville, toward the Salmon River canyon.

Holy shit. The smoke column rising from the canyon was huge and looked angry. I switched my fire department radio from pager to open radio, so I could hear the radio traffic. Nothing, not a damn thing on the radio – but, I knew with that volume of smoke this early in the day, the situation could not be good. So much for a typical Sunday, I thought. Finishing a quick breakfast, I started preparing, getting ready to go to war with fire. While checking my fire gear bags, I began reminiscing about how fire had burned its way into my life.

A Young Boy and Fire

We lived on the western edge of Santa Barbara, with a five-mile stretch of farms and orchards between our house and the small southern California town of Goleta. One evening just about dusk my dad, who had fought fires before I was born, walked me up to a little hill just a short distance from our house.

Dad had worked for three summers on both the fire crew and engine crew on the Los Padres National Forest outside of Santa Barbara. He spent a short time with Santa Barbara County Fire Department as well, but then moved into a different career. He was still interested in monitoring local fires, even if he was no longer able to fight fire himself.

The major north-south highway, US 101, was a mile from our place, and I could hear sirens coming from the highway, traveling northwest. When Dad and I looked to the west we could see an entire hillside aglow in orange and red. In a short time, I was caught like a deer in the headlights, mesmerized by the red-orange hills and orange-brown sky above. As we watched the hillside, it seemed alive with dancing flames gobbling up acre after acre in just minutes. We watched until it was a little past my bedtime. That first fire I remember was called the Refugio Fire, and in September, 1955, it burned 77,000 acres in 10 days – the entire coastal side of the Santa Ynez Mountains. It was estimated that during the height of the winds, the fire burned 41,000 acres in a 30-hour time period. It was stopped a few miles from our home after burning the canyons behind Goleta.

In reviewing some stories regarding this fire, I found mention of some firefighters hearing explosions where there should not have been explosions. The Refugio Fire, in its rampage toward the Pacific Ocean, burned over an unexploded shell or two hidden in the brush, according to *History of the Santa Barbara County Fire Department* by Robert J.

Moseley.

In 1942, during the early stages of the Pacific Theatre of World War II, the Japanese sent a submarine on a bold attempt to put fear into the Americans. In a relatively narrow stretch of land between the Pacific Ocean and the Santa Ynez Mountains, and between the towns of Goleta and Gaviota, there is a small community called Ellwood. Ellwood consisted of a school, a few homes, an oil refinery with storage tanks, and numerous offshore and onshore oil wells. The Japanese submarine I-17 approached the Ellwood area and fired a number of shells, trying to hit the storage tanks.

In an account of this shelling found in California State Military Department records, reference is made to a 1982 *Parade* magazine article suggesting the captain of the Japanese submarine, Commander Nishino Kozo, had an axe to grind regarding the Ellwood refinery. As captain of a Japanese oil tanker in the late 1930's, Kozo had visited the Ellwood refinery; during his walk from the beach to a welcoming ceremony, he fell butt first into some prickly pear cactus – to the amusement of the refinery workers. On the evening of February 23, 1942, Commander Kozo's submarine crew took about 35 minutes to fire upwards of 24 shells at the oil facilities. With his dignity now repaired, Commander Kozo and his submarine left the area – after causing one injury and less than $500 in damage.

Fire has seemed to be a part of me for most of my life – it was always there somehow. We lived close to the city limits and about 1¼ miles from the nearest Santa Barbara City fire station, to the east. To the west about 2½ miles away was a Santa Barbara County fire station. A fire call near us would often bring both the red Santa Barbara City engine as well as the white Santa Barbara County engine. When I was about 5 years old, my dad had a bad asthma attack, and the first emergency crew to arrive was a red fire engine. My sister, one year younger than I, my 2-year-old brother, and I stood in fascination at the living room window watching the firemen carrying boxes of stuff into our home. Grandma Sangster happened to be arriving at this moment. She saw the fire truck and firefighters in front of our house, then saw her three grandchildren at the window, and quickly assessed the situation. She was a stout woman of German and French descent, with a no-nonsense, "you had better do what I say or you will hurt" attitude. She was going to rescue her grandchildren – since the firemen were not – and she went into running-back mode. Grandma pushed a couple of firemen out of her way as she hurried through the front door and into the living room. Mom was finally able to subdue her with the reality of the situation, and Grandma calmed down enough to chat and make sure her son and grandchildren were all right. We all thought it was funny, but only after Grandma had left.

When I turned 11 years old, I became a newspaper carrier for a route that included a trailer park, apartments, and homes within a few blocks of our house. The newspaper publisher preferred to hire young delivery people, so quite a few of us in the same age group had jobs.

While still in grade school, my brothers and I would sneak into the lemon grove across the street, or into the avocado orchard behind us or the orange grove just up the street. We played like we were explorers, finding a new continent never set foot on before. Or we'd play war, pretending to be in the European forest or the jungle of a South Pacific island. My parents were strict, and we were told not to pick any fruit – that was someone's living, and we had no right to steal.

Progress came to our little haven though, and these natural fruit baskets were replaced by apartments, banks, and gas stations. I was serious about my job of delivering newspapers; I'd get home from school and sit on the cement wall in front of the house and wait for the newspaper van to show up with my bundles of newspapers.

One day while waiting on the wall, I happened to be looking across the street at the new apartment complex under construction. Something caught my eye while staring at the wood frame structure. A wisp of what looked like smoke tendriled up from the open frame structure. Watching a little longer, I became sure it was smoke, and I ran in and told Mom. She called the fire department. I dashed back out to watch, and it didn't take long for the fire engines to show up and quickly put the fire out. A little while later the captain saw me sitting on the wall and walked over. He asked if I had reported the fire. He told me that a hot rivet had set a framing stud to smoldering, and that everyone had gone home from the job site. He said if I hadn't spotted it when I did, there would have been a much more serious fire.

The fun places for kids around Santa Barbara were only about five miles from my home, so we did a lot of bicycling. With the money from my paper route, I purchased a specially made Schwinn bicycle built for the rigors of the paper carrier. It had an extra-heavy-duty suspension, a newspaper bag carrier over the back wheel, and a two-speed shift operated by foot action instead of the normally hand-operated shifter. Whenever we could get permission from our parents, a few of us older kids would bike to Stearn's wharf to fish or over to Henry's beach to play in the sand – or we'd head to Goleta to watch the airplanes.

The airport for the Santa Barbara area was at Goleta, and the U.S. Forest Service (USFS) had an air attack base there. During the fire season, I would ride my bike the six miles to the airport to watch and visit a little with the pilots of the "borate bombers" as we called them then. Many of these planes were built for duty during World War II, but were now specially adapted to haul a liquid slurry of water and borate or bentonite clay.

Back in 1934, Howard Flint of the USFS had an idea to "water bomb" a fire. After several trial runs by the famous Johnson brothers (Johnson Air Service) out of Missoula, Montana, the idea was shelved because of problems in getting a reasonable amount of water onto the fire. (See *Tall Timber Pilots* by Dick White and Larry Florek, Viking Press, 1953.)

In 1955, Forest Fire Control Officer Joe Ely had asked the Nolta Brothers in Willows, California, if they could modify a cropdusting airplane for firefighting, and they did – the Stearman. Nolta designed a dump valve, or gate, and the means to yank it open for a drop and mounted it in his No. 1 Stearman, 75 Kaydet. Even though the plane could carry only a hundred gallons of water, Vance Nolta, the pilot, was able to hit targets with good accuracy. Nolta's Stearman dropped water on the Mendenhall Fire that summer, and aerial firefighting was born. An excellent discussion of this successful beginning of aerial firefighting was written by Joe Ely (*How It Was*, Joe Ely, provided by George Nolta from the collection of Irene Nolta).

The word of this new tool in the fight against wildfire spread almost as quickly as a wildfire, and just a year later there were seven modified biplanes working on wildfires. These first pilots of the aerial program were gutsy, and through their efforts and ideas, the program grew to using larger aircraft and mixing water with additives to make the moisture do a better job in helping to retard the progress of a fire. Today we refer to fire fighting airplanes as airtankers, and now they carry a liquid fertilizer instead of the water and clay mix of years ago.

Usually, the Goleta Air Attack Base had two aircraft assigned to it during fire season: a TBM and a F7F. The TBM was a naval single-engine torpedo bomber called the Avenger during World War II. It was modified to carry a missile, hence the acronym TBM, for Torpedo Bomber Missile. The TBM was heavy and slow, but it was a powerful aircraft. You could hear the roar of the engine at takeoff from six miles away.

The F7F was a fast twin-engine fighter that had just started to fly missions when World War II ended. Called the Tigercat, this fighter was capable of awesome speeds for those days. The fuselage was narrow, designed as a fast fighter instead of a bomber. A special tank to carry the fire retardant had to be mounted to the outside, giving the underside of the Tigercat a distinctive bulge – and thus slowing down the Tigercat. Yet even with this limitation it could still get a load of retardant to the fire quickly.

During a large fire, there would be several airplanes working out of the Goleta base. It was not unusual to see three TBMs, a couple of F7Fs, a twin-engine PBY Catalina flying boat, and a couple of the four-engine B-17 heavy bombers flying loads of retardant out of Goleta. After numerous visits to the fence of the air attack base, I got to know the pilots a little; sometimes the F7F pilot would even wag his wings over our house on the way back from a fire.

On my paper delivery route was a mobile home park of senior citizens. Some of the residents would call upon me to help them with various chores. I quickly grew to hate vinegar, and still do, but had to admit that vinegar and newspaper cleaned windows quite well! Thanks to these numerous chores, I had some spending money. My parents made sure that a large percentage of the money I earned went into a savings account. The little bit I had left I could spend on what I wanted. There was a popular series of small metal toys called Matchbox, and a series of plastic military toys the same size as the Matchbox vehicles. I accumulated a few of these great toys as well as few model airplanes I built from kits. I even had models of the Avenger and the Tigercat painted to match the retardant planes at the Goleta airbase.

We had a two-car-wide carport with a workshop at the end, and behind that was a small slope of maybe 30 feet up to a wooden fence. I would set up my toys and soldiers and pretend there was a wildfire, and I'd move the toys around to attack the fire. One day, I got this dumb-ass idea of using gasoline to start a little fire and make this pretend war a bit more real. After pouring gasoline onto the green grass, I lit it off. This was more like it! One afternoon, though, after I'd run this carefully orchestrated use of fire a couple times, Dad drove into the carport early and smelled smoke. I was busted and not able to sit for a few days. Sure never tried that stunt again, at least, not until years later after I became a firefighter and had to start fires for legitimate purposes.

While in Boy Scouts, we made a number of trips outside

the Santa Barbara area. A main camp for much of the Southern California Boy Scout troops was some 35 miles from Santa Barbara on the Los Padres National Forest. We spent many weekends at the camp learning outdoor skills. Since Santa Barbara is along the Pacific Coast, just above sea level, snow was rare and then usually above the 3000-foot elevation. For a snow trip, the Scouts would travel in station wagons to the high country out of Ojai, where the snow lasted longer than just a few hours.

On one of these early spring snow trips, we left Santa Barbara during a warm, dry spell and spent a fun time in the snow at Mt. Frazier. The next day, we headed back to Santa Barbara and noticed the still smoking, blackened remnants of a fire outside Carpenteria, a small town east of Santa Barbara. The story behind this fire was quite a tale, but said to be true – a hawk had grabbed a snake to feed its young, but the snake had other plans. During the fight, the snake was dropped by the hawk. It fell onto a powerline causing the lines to arc and sparking a grass fire. The air was very unstable. A dust devil hit that growing grass fire and sent it whirling into thick brush. Soon the fire had created its own vortex wind. This fire whorl quickly grew in intensity, lifting and throwing stuff in its path. There was a newspaper story about some sailors on a ship about 16 miles off the coast of Carpenteria who claimed they were bombarded by burnt chickens. These chickens would have been from the chicken coop that was in the path of this fire vortex. The fire quickly ran out of fuel when it burned to the edge of a green polo field. The vortex fell flat allowing the firefighters to get the upper hand.

It was on September 22, 1964, when fire visited Santa Barbara with a demonic streak. I was just back to school after a week-long absence caused by a bout of ear infections. Having an ear infection was no fun, and the pain was unbearable. (My poor mother not only had me to deal with, but one of my brothers was also sick with an ear infection at the same time). I had to continue taking medicine while at school, and as I was excused and left the classroom for a drink of water, I heard the F7F Tigercat fly over the school heading east toward the Montecito area. As I watched the airtanker go over, I wondered where the fire was. Because the F7F returned quickly, I figured the fire must not be too far away. By the time school was out I could see a column of smoke to the east.

Early that evening, after listening to the news, Dad loaded us into the car and drove toward Montecito to see what the fire was doing and where it was burning. The area of Montecito and the "Riviera" where it was burning was a nightmare maze of narrow roads and steep driveways. Dad wanted to make sure we were quite a distance from the fire, not only to keep out of the way of the firefighting efforts, but also for our safety. It was tough trying to find a safe place from which to view the fire, but we found an open area where we could see it from a distance. The Montecito area, home to movie stars and millionaires, was getting the brunt of the fire's voracious appetite.

From our view point we could see the white lights of the city in the foreground. In the background, along the edge of the city lights, were orange-red dancing lights. Some of these orange-red lights would remain stationary, while most of the others would be moving closer to the city lights. Whenever the dense smoke would clear we could see a wall of these pulsating flames. I did not know at that time that the stationary orange-red lights, the flames that were not moving, were homes being destroyed. Even though we were quite a distance from the flames, we could see embers falling near us, blown by the Santa Ana winds.

The next day the fire continued on its rampage; the changing winds were pushing it in all directions. Numerous homes in the Montecito foothills had been burned, but the toll so far was not as bad as it could have been. The Santa Ana winds had died down, and that second night, the fire decided it had had enough of the Montecito area. The fire turned in the opposite direction heading north along the mountain range that forms the northern edge of Santa

Barbara.

Dad had been watching the news and looking out the window. He let me stay up a little later than normal this particular night. The fire had raced up to the top of the ridge behind Santa Barbara and jumped the road on top of the ridge called East El Camino Cielo. This headed the fire away from Santa Barbara, into the back country behind the Santa Ynez mountains. This was good for Santa Barbara but bad for the USFS. The fire was heading toward a huge expanse of brush and timber that hadn't burned since the 220,000-acre Matilija Fire in 1932. Noticing the Santa Ana winds picking up again, Dad predicted the fire would jump back to the Santa Barbara side of the mountains, and I went off to bed with the view of the fire miles away.

Weather records show that at around 2 a.m. the air was a hot 92 degrees, the humidity barely 10 percent, with the Santa Anas blowing at 35 miles per hour and more. Shortly after 2 a.m,. Dad woke me and said he needed my help. I looked out the window and was aghast. Instead of the fire being miles away to the east where I saw it before going to bed, the fire was now about 1½ miles north of us, between our house and the mountains! Because of the heavy smoke, I couldn't see all of the fire, but I could see enough of the brown orange glow to know it was bad, very bad. Dad said he had to take the dump truck up the street and help people evacuate, and I needed to stay and watch things around the house. We were not too worried about our place; we had 22 acres of green grass around us. But, there were areas of dry weeds at the outskirts of the green grass, and a few burning embers were coming down. Fortunately for us, the winds were pushing the fire to the west past us, instead of to the south, toward us. A few hours later the winds died down, and the fire lost its appetite for a while.

By early morning I could see smoke coming up from all along the hillside just up the street from our place. Later that morning, a very tired and grimy Dad showed up and told us what had happened. He'd arrived at a friend's house to help them evacuate when a firestorm hit. The house next door had become a fireball. The friend dropped everything and panicked, trying to get up onto the roof of his house to save it from the same fate as the neighbor's house. With Dad's fire experience, he knew this was not the place to be; he grabbed his friend, steered him to the truck, and they drove out to a safer area. When they were let back into the area later that day, there was only one house destroyed in that subdivision – the one caught in the initial firestorm during the evacuation.

The fire managers decided to try to keep this wicked fire from jumping Highway 154, a two-lane paved road over the mountain leading into the Santa Ynez valley. Crews started backfires along the east side of the highway, while other crews along the top of the mountains were poised to hold the fire from slopping over into the back country. The winds switched and pushed the fire to the top of the mountains where it jumped the fireline. The fire was gobbling up acres and acres of brush and oak trees, heading toward the USFS Los Prietos Ranger Station and the quaint community of Paradise. The Forest Service officer in charge of this division was a good friend of Dad's from the days Dad worked with him 14 years before. He was experienced in using fire against fire, backfiring to stop a raging fire. He grabbed the few firefighters he had and started running backfires around the Ranger Station and the nearby buildings. The backfires saved the buildings and the Ranger Station, and crews were able to hold the fire in check in this area.

A few days later, when it was safe to go into the Montecito area, Dad took us to one of the famous mansions where an aunt of his worked as a maid. The mansion property had its own polo field, and as we drove up the cobblestone driveway, we saw the that the polo field had been transformed into a war camp with 50 or more fire engines parked there. As a young boy, I couldn't care less about seeing how the rich and famous lived – I wanted to be walking around that fire camp seeing up close the fabulous array of firefighting equipment. We were treated to a tour of the mansion, but my mind was out there on the polo field. Firefighters had saved the mansion, stopping the fire as it roared up to the back of the six-car garage. This fire, called the Coyote Fire, killed one firefighter, and burned 150 homes and 67,000 acres.

The following spring a couple of my best friends went with me on an overnight hike into the burned area. Although we saw blackened skeletons of oak trees and chaparral stubs a few inches out of the ground, we also saw green. With the winter rains, the grasses were sprouting, and there were islands of unburned areas scattered around. Mother Nature was at work rejuvenating the burned area.

Hotshots

Damn I still hadn't heard any radio traffic regarding the fire, and it had been over an hour since I'd first seen the huge smoke column. During a fire call we'd had in Grangeville the day before, I had learned from one of my fellow Grangeville Fire Department volunteers that there was a wildfire burning in the Lucile area 30 miles south of us. Because I was also a volunteer assistant chief for the Salmon River Rural Fire Department, responsible for homes in the Lucile area, I was worried. If the fire was burning close to homes there, I should be there to help. But nobody had called me, and I did not want to drive to the fire and "freelance."

Freelancing is a dirty word in firefighting. It refers to someone who is working alone and without a plan. It's frowned upon and worse – those who do it are quickly branded and black-listed. Most importantly, it's dangerous – it risks lives. No serious professional firefighter, from their first year on, has any use for a freelancer – under any circumstances.

Despite my motivation to go help, I knew I needed to wait for orders and thus be a viable resource and not a "loose cannon" on the incident. I used my waiting time to get a couple of computers ready for customer pickup on Monday morning – my "real job", that of a computer repair tech. While trying to concentrate on these two computers, my mind wandered back to the days when I had first started fighting wildfires. It seemed like only yesterday.

In February of 1970, when I was 18, I worked up enough courage to interview for a job with the U.S. Forest Service, something I had wanted to do for years. The headquarters for the Los Padres National Forest was close by in Goleta, and I visited the Fire Management Officer (FMO) for the Forest and presented my job references. The FMO had jurisdiction over everything regarding fire on the Los Padres National Forest; he'd been there for many years. He was praised for his work as a line officer during the Coyote Fire of 1964, and was credited with helping save the lives of a crew trapped and burned over on the Coyote Fire.

Once the Forest FMO learned I was the son of Bill Sangster, whom he remembered from twenty years ago, we spent part of the interview talking about Dad and how he had worked with the Los Prietos Hotshot Crew, the crew I wanted to be a part of. The next thing I knew, the Forest FMO was on the phone with the hotshot crew foreman telling him he had an applicant for the crew. After an interview with the foreman and submitting the paperwork, I had a job with the Los Prietos Hotshot Crew. I was ecstatic!

In those days, the ultimate wildland firefighters were the smokejumpers, followed closely by the hotshot crews. Michael Thoele, in his book *Fireline: Summer Battles of The West* (Fulcrum Publishing, 1995), describes hotshots as "in paramilitary terms, the Marines, gung-ho ground pounders charging up the beach against stacked odds." I was in the clouds, riding high with the notion that in a few months I would finally be doing what I had been waiting nearly fifteen years for. Here it was June 16, 1970, and the eighteen members of the Los Prietos Hotshot Crew came together at last.

The term hotshot was derived from the fact that these special crews were sent into the hottest parts of the fire. The first hotshot crews, the El Cariso and Del Rosa Hotshots, were organized in 1947, in Southern California. The quick success of this project led to the development of more crews, and in 1949, the Los Prietos Hotshot Crew was started and initially tasked by the U.S. Flood Project to protect the Santa Ynez watershed. As Ray Ford wrote in the *Santa Barbara Independent* newspaper (Sept. 30, 2009), this crew grew into "one of the most well honed and professional firefighting forces anywhere." The crew was based at the Los Prietos Ranger Station, in a pleasant little valley called Paradise, a thirty-mile drive over the Santa Ynez Mountains from Santa Barbara.

In the past, all of the crew members were required to live in the barracks on the grounds of the ranger station. The barracks were built in 1953, to house thirty-five members of the hotshot crew. In 1965, the size of the crew was cut back to twenty, and the crew members were still required to stay in the barracks. A recent change in policy had allowed those crew members who wished to commute from Santa Barbara every day to do so – as long as they could be back to the Ranger Station within two hours. For all of us on the crew, whether staying in Santa Barbara or in the barracks, we had to either be close to a phone or make sure someone knew where to find us quickly.

I decided to stay in the barracks instead of doing the sixty-mile roundtrip mountainous drive every day, I ended up bunking with two other crew members: one from Baltimore, Maryland and the other from the Compton area of Los Angeles. Normally, the Los Prietos Hotshot Crew consisted of twenty firefighters, but in 1970, our crew was short-changed and had just fifteen firefighters, two squad bosses, and the crew foreman. John (from Baltimore) and I were the smallest members of the crew, while the rest of the crew included a couple of high school football players maintaining their strength and agility during the summer while getting paid, a few young men just wanting to experience the thrill of fighting fire, and a few who had been on the crew before. A couple of these football players were huge. One we nicknamed Baby Huey after the cartoon character in Donald Duck episodes.

Our barracks was in good shape, with a kitchen facility we

could use to cook our own meals. We had to keep everything clean, and had inspections similar to the military. The only problem we ever had was an ant attack. I remember one morning pouring a bowl of sugar-frosted flakes and ending up with a bowl full of ants crawling around the flakes. Lost my appetite, and then did a major clean on the kitchen.

Standard procedure for hotshot crews was a minimum of sixteen hours of specialized training covering the use of hand tools and saws for fireline building, safety, fire behavior and weather, use of water, safety around helicopters, and behavior expected of a top-level crew. During the work day, we were expected to wear either jeans or Frisco black work pants, regular top Vibram sole lace-up boots, cotton undershorts and undershirt, heavy boot socks, a long-sleeve tan cotton work shirt, and heavy-duty leather work gloves. We had to furnish these items ourselves. I couldn't afford a pair of the popular White's boots that many firefighters wore, so I bought a pair of Red Wings. These boots barely made it through the summer, and if I had skipped college and stayed on, I would have needed another pair of boots.

A special fire shirt made of Nomex, a fire-resistant material, and a metal hard hat were issued to us. The orange-colored Nomex shirts were expensive, so we were each issued only one and wore it only while on a working fire.

In addition, we were issued web gear, war bag, and a fire shelter. Our web gear consisted of a military surplus fanny pack, clamped onto a wide belt called a web belt that went around the waist. A set of suspenders was clamped to the web belt to help support the weight, which often included two one-quart canteens, a full fanny pack, and a fire shelter attached to the belt. Inside the fanny pack, we carried a personalized first aid kit, headlight, extra batteries, and some type of rain gear or light jacket. Sometimes we would toss in a box of C-rats or at least part of a box.

The C rations, as they were properly called, were dinners in a box. They came in handy when real food was not available. The rations included such tasty treats in cans as tuna casserole, beef stew, spaghetti, or beef hash. Along with the main entrée, there was also an Army green can of a dessert, usually tins of crackers, tins of jelly or peanut butter, and a packet with a can opener, coffee, hot chocolate mix, sugar, and salt. It usually worked out fairly well in dividing up a case of the rations among the crew. Most of the guys did not like the pecan cake roll dessert, nor did they like the cold tuna casserole. I liked the pecan cake roll better than the dry pound cake and found the cold tuna easier on my stomach than cold spaghetti, hash, or stew.

Eating the C-rats was a production, kind of a last-ditch effort at getting food. First, one had to open the tin cans, and no one had room in their fanny pack to carry a real can opener. The P38 can opener that was supposed to be included with each meal was about an inch long with a folding blade about the size of a fingernail. Very quickly, we found that keeping a P38 attached to our key chain was a good idea, as some kits came without one. It took a while to open a can with something that small, but hunger made one proficient, and soon we could open a can very quickly.

In addition to the web gear, we carried a large pack called a war bag; it held our change of socks and underwear, extra clothes for the trip home, personal hygiene items, a coat, and a sleeping bag. The war bag was our limited apparel resupply and usually was left behind in the fire camp or on the crew truck and was not carried with us on the fireline.

Our transportation consisted of a 1960's cab-over International Loadstar flatbed truck, Forest Service green and gray in color. We sat seven to a side, facing each other, our backs up against the metal compartments. We built wooden storage boxes and put them on top of the metal compartments along each side of the crew carrier; in this way we could store our web gear behind us and grab it as we were getting off the truck instead of wasting time trying to get our gear from inside the compartments. We had a military surplus canvas top mounted over the crew carrier, which gave us some relief from the wind and weather. We could roll up the back and sides for air, or roll them down during a cold night's drive or a rain shower. On the outside of both sides of the crew carrier was a large red and white emblem with the words *Incendi Proeliatores*, which (roughly translated) means fire soldiers or "fighter of fires."

The Crew also had a pickup truck called a chase truck, which usually carried the foreman and our firefighting tools. One of the squad bosses or the foreman drove the pickup while the other squad boss drove the crew truck with one of the crew members riding shotgun.

We'd had one and a half days of training, and we were finishing our lunch on the second day. We were told to load up into the trucks, because we were needed to work a fire that had just started near Santa Maria, about an hour's drive north. We were all looking at each other saying "Yeah right," must be part of the training because we haven't finished training yet. So, we headed out for what we thought was a pretend fire, eager to finish our training. We wanted to get to fight a real fire. As we approached Santa Maria, though, we could see the column of smoke. We decided the training session was going to be quite practical. Cool, our first flames! We had heard about hotshot crew training sessions in years past in which the crew was sent to Camp Roberts or Fort Hunter Liggett to the north of us – and they practiced with real fire. Perhaps this was going to be the same sort of thing.

We pulled onto a flat piece of ground just off the highway where numerous fire engines and vehicles were parked, with the fire some distance ahead and up the hillside. This parking area was called a staging area, and it was here we started to realize that perhaps this was *not* pretend. The look of the fire, and the actions of the firefighters scattered around the staging area, told us that this was real. Our crew foreman headed to the command post to get the assignment while we disembarked from our crew truck and grabbed our fire gear.

As we unloaded, the foreman gathered the squad bosses together and passed along what the fire boss was expecting of the crew. We were divided up into two squads, and our squad bosses told us what was in store, what we needed to accomplish, and which safety concerns we needed to be mindful of. We were assigned hand tools, and we unloaded tools from the chase truck. The whole thing was like a blur, happening quickly, and some of us were not really prepared for this. We were led to an open area of the field to a waiting Bell 47 helicopter. This was getting cool now, as I had never ridden in a helicopter before.

The Bell 47 is a small helicopter with two seats – one for the pilot and one for a passenger. It was made famous in the Korean War and was seen by millions of TV watchers of the M*A*S*H episodes. During firefighting situations, the Bell 47 doors are removed for quick loading and unloading. To get us onto the fire quickly, the helitack crew would put two in the passenger seat if possible. While we waited to load, a helitack crew member would ask our weight, trying to get the best weight load mix and not overload the helicopter.

We were briefed on approaching and leaving helicopters safely. We were warned to approach only from the front, the pilot's 10 o'clock through 2 o'clock view so the pilot could see us. We made sure our hard hats and anything we were wearing were strapped securely – the last thing we wanted to do was ruin a multi-million-dollar aircraft by having a loose item fly up and chip the blades, or worse yet, cause a crash.

When the helitack crew member had fit us in, he strapped our tools to the cargo basket on the outside of the helicopter. Since I was small, I was placed on the outside of the passenger seat and strapped in. After taking off and gaining altitude to get above some powerlines, we banked to the right, the side I was dangling from, and the view from my side was phenomenal. What a rush! I quickly became convinced that riding in a helicopter was much preferred over hiking.

We arrived at the helispot, which was cleared for safe landing and takeoff, and we unloaded. We met up with the rest of the waiting crew, and then, lined up according to the hand tool we were assigned and the plan of attack.

During our brief training prior to this first fire, we had been introduced to the use of hand tools and chainsaws in the construction of fireline. The procedure for building line was to follow the foreman or squad boss as he marked where the fireline was to be built. The foreman usually took off in front and used flagging tape or cut branches to mark where he wanted the fireline built. Usually, one of the crew members followed next with a brush hook to hack away branches and open a small path for the chainsaws.

The brush hook was my favorite tool. During many of the fires we worked on, I was lead brush hook, working ahead of the chainsaws. The brush hook was basically a curved piece of sharpened steel at the end of a heavy-duty wooden handle. The objective was to cut branches or small trunks with the curve of the hook. If done right, one could slice through a small tree trunk in one swing. The end of the hook was also useful in gathering up cut branches to get them out of the way.

Both chainsaws would follow next. One of the saws had a straight bar for cutting logs, trees, and thicker brush. The other chainsaw had a bow bar, in which the chain ran around a wide hollowed-out bar with a stinger on the end. The bow bar was a lighter weight system which could cut brush faster than the straight bar, but the bow bar was much more dangerous to use. One of our crew had to visit the emergency room to get a chainsaw cut in his leg sewn shut. The problem was the hollow center of the bow bar, and the way the cut brush fell into the hollow.

Saw operators wore special chaps to protect them from the waist down to the tops of their boots. Should a chainsaw jerk back and hit you, the chaps would absorb the cutting blades. In the case of the bow bar, you had to be careful when jerking the saw to clear out the branches in the bow; unless you were short like me, the chaps left a little gap between the top of the boots and the bottom of the chaps. For some reason, the bow bar would zero in on this area and the results were not pretty. Not only was the cut operator hurt, but the crew was now short at least two firefighters: the hurt one and the other one who was helping the injured firefighter to a first aid station or an EMT on the line. Usually, each chainsaw had both an operator and a swamper who cleared away the cut material, so the saw operator did not have to stop and put down the saw to do his own clearing.

After the chainsaws cut as much brush as quickly as possible, then another brush hook would follow to clean up any uncut brush. Next came three to five Pulaskis, a great tool for chopping, digging, and trenching.

The Pulaski is basically a combination hoe and axe, and it is named after a U.S. Forest Service employee who designed it. The Pulaski is handy for chopping trees or brush, digging roots, and for making sure your fireline has reached what is called mineral soil, which means just plain dirt with nothing burnable mixed in.

Ranger Ed Pulaski is credited with saving the lives of all but five of his 45-man crew during the 1910 Big Burn – the "Big Burn" included over 1,700 fires that burned over 3 million acres across northern Idaho and western Montana. At least 85 people were killed. Ranger Pulaski held his crew at gunpoint inside a mine tunnel while the fire raged outside. He redesigned a tool that was being used for trail maintenance. Wildland firefighters soon found it especially useful and nicknamed the tool 'Pulaski' in honor of Ranger Pulaski.

We are taught that there are three types of burnable fuels we needed to deal with: above ground, on the ground, and below the ground. When building a fireline, you not only have to remove the burnable stuff above ground, you also have to make sure the stuff on the ground and under the ground is not able to carry fire across your line.

In some parts of the country, the McLeod tool will follow next. The McLeod is a combination wide-blade hoe and rake. "The McLeod tool was designed by USFS Ranger Malcolm McLeod of the Sierra National Forest. It has a large hoe-like blade on one side and a tined blade like a rake on the other. It is used for fighting wildland fires and trail building. It was originally intended for raking firelines with the teeth and for cutting branches and sod with the sharpened hoe edge. It is useful for removing slough and berm from a trail and tamping or compacting a trail. Because of its shape, it can be used to shape a trail's backslope. It is awkward to transport or store and originally had a removable handle." (from *Window on the Clearwater*, Nancy and Mike Butler). In certain areas the firefighter using a McLeod can make quick work of removing duff, such as pine needles, grass, or small branches. The McLeod also makes a great tool for dragging debris away using the rake portion of the tool, so we usually had a couple of McCleods following the Pulaskis.

Bringing up the rear of the line building effort are the shovels. We used "Lady Shovels," which feature a narrower blade and a shorter handle than what you find at the hardware store. These were used to widen and clear the fireline, and to throw dirt onto burning material close to the line. We kept the shovel blade sharp for those times we needed to use it for chopping branches or roots missed by the Pulaskis and McLeods.

After all our crew members were accounted for and the helicopter had left for another task, we started walking to the area requiring line building. The fire was burning in a draw and was too hot for a direct attack, so we were building line in what is called an indirect attack, a distance away from the heat and flames. Because we were working with the fire below us and we couldn't see the fire, one of the squad bosses was assigned as a lookout; he watched from a vantage point to see what the fire was doing.

The most important aspect of firefighting is safety. After numerous tragic deaths of firefighters, rules of engagement were developed – a critical part of our training. These rules include the 10 Standard Firefighting Orders and the 18 Watchout Situations, all developed after studying the deaths of firefighters in fires such as the Griffith Park Fire of 1933, in which at least 25 firefighters were killed; the Blackwater

Fire in 1937 where 15 firefighters were killed; the Hauser Creek Fire of 1943 in which 11 firefighters were killed; the Mann Gulch Fire of 1949 during which 13 firefighters were killed; the Rattlesnake Fire in 1953 at which 15 firefighters were killed; the Inaja Fire of 1956 in which 11 firefighters were killed; the Loop Fire of 1966 during which 12 firefighters were killed; and the Canyon Fire in 1968 in which eight firefighters died. We had these rules printed on bright yellow material attached to our hard hats, and we constantly went over the rules. The 10 Standard Orders are:

1. Keep informed on fire weather conditions and forecasts.
2. Know what your fire is doing at all times.
3. Base all actions on current and expected behavior of the fire.
4. Identify escape routes and safety zones and make them known.
5. Post lookouts when there is possible danger.
6. Be alert. Keep calm. Think clearly. Act decisively.
7. Maintain prompt communications with your forces, your supervisor, and adjoining forces.
8. Give clear instructions and ensure they are understood.
9. Maintain control of your forces at all times.
10. Fight fire aggressively, having provided for safety first.

The 18 Watchout Situations are:

1. Fire not scouted and sized up.
2. In country not seen in daylight.
3. Safety zones and escape routes not identified.
4. Unfamiliar with weather and local factors influencing fire behavior.
5. Uninformed on strategy, tactics, and hazards.

6. Instructions and assignments not clear.
7. No communication link with crewmembers/supervisors.
8. Constructing line without safe anchor point.
9. Building fireline downhill with fire below.
10. Attempting frontal assault on fire.
11. Unburned fuel between you and the fire.
12. Cannot see main fire, not in contact with anyone who can.
13. On a hillside where rolling material can ignite fuel below.
14. Weather is getting hotter and drier.
15. Wind increases and/or changes direction.
16. Getting frequent spot fires across line.
17. Terrain and fuels make escape to safety zones difficult.
18. Taking a nap near the fireline.

We were reminded that these Watchouts were warnings, and that each of us was responsible to see that we as a crew operated as safely as possible under the circumstances. If we could not be completely safe, then we should work to mitigate the situation. So, while we were building fireline in thick brush, not able to see the fire approaching us, the foreman mitigated the danger by assigning a lookout to watch the fire and let him know what the fire was doing.

Each of us carried a fire shelter. This device is a specially developed aluminum foil tent designed to shelter firefighters if the fire overwhelms them so quickly that they are unable to reach a safety zone. We jokingly called these fire shelters "shake'n'bake", because we would swelter inside on a hot Southern California afternoon during a practice deployment.

The fire shelter was originally developed in Australia in 1958, and by 1960, the Missoula Equipment Development Center of the USFS started working with ideas for firefighter protection. Out of this process came the first mass production of fire shelters in 1967 (from *History of the Development of the Fire Shelter*, Dick Mangan, 2003). We practiced deploying shelters till we could do it in less than 35 seconds, from clearing a spot to laying down in the tent.

As a firefighter, you always look for an area of safety and a safe means of getting there quickly. If the fire turns on you and you can't get to the safety zone, then you must quickly find an area clear of heavy fuels, as wide a clearing as possible, and on as flat a piece of ground as possible. You need to clear any fuels such as dry grass from the area, then quickly take off your web gear and grab the fire shelter pack. After ripping open the buttoned cover and grabbing the tightly packed shelter, you pull the tab to open the protective case and pull out the accordion-folded aluminum shelter. After throwing it open, you face the fire and step into the foot straps while grabbing the hand straps. The wind from the advancing fire will help open the shelter; you then quickly turn and fall to the ground face first, feet to the fire. You want to make sure you have a canteen of water in the shelter with you, and make sure the shelter edges are on the ground with no gaps. Then, you wait and try to suppress the panic.

During practice we had to stay put in the shelter until the foreman or squad boss gave the okay to crawl out. In many training sessions, while we were lying inside the shelter, one of the squad bosses would come along and grab hold of the shelter and shake it to see if you had a good hold on the shelter straps. The lesson was to be prepared for fierce winds that could tear your shelter away from you.

It is common among wildland firefighters today to recognize that when firefighters have to deploy a fire shelter, someone probably screwed up. Unlike the macho days of the late '60's and early '70's where we pushed the fire hard and relied on the shelter as a fallback, today the emphasis is on a safety zone close by so everyone can move into it in case of a problem.

With the lookout in place, our crew started building line. We were getting on-the-job training, and thank goodness there were a few crew members with previous experience to help us newbies! The object was to build the least possible line necessary to hold the fire; the rule of thumb was to build fireline as wide as 1½ times the height of the burning vegetation. So if we were working in a field of 12-inch grass, the fireline was to be 18 inches wide. However, most of our fires were in brush, which could be 10 to 14 feet high, which meant a fireline of 15 to 20 feet wide. Fortunately in most cases we would cut a 5 to 8 foot wide line to mineral soil, then cut down the brush on either side of the line the remaining 10 feet or so. If we could get in against the fire, we could build an even narrower fireline, using the black as part of the line width.

We had a method of line production that worked to not only put line down quickly but also safely. Each firefighter would maintain about a 10- foot spacing between him and the guy in front of him. Once you worked that 10-foot section, whether you were sawing, chopping, scraping, digging, or trenching, then you approached the firefighter in front of you and yelled "bump!" This meant everyone would move forward and take over the remaining section in front, maintaining the 10-foot spacing. After some practice, you were able to determine how much you should do to your section of line.

After safety came speed – you didn't want to spend too much time making bare dirt. With other Pulaskis in the mix, for example, you might need to clear only a portion of the 10-foot section because you were just one of three Pulaskis, and each took a chunk of the work. With the McCleods and shovels following, you could adjust your work and speed. We could tell how eager or how tired the crew was by how quickly and loudly the bumps came. Teamwork was especially important in line construction, and you quickly learned that the lives of the crew depended upon our ability to work quickly and safely. We soon learned to pace ourselves, because we had no idea how long we were going to be swinging.

The sounds of battle now included helicopters and airtankers overhead, dozers pushing over brush and trees and scraping fireline, wildland engines pumping water to nozzles at the end of strung-out fire hoses, and now the added sounds of our crew with its two chainsaws, the chopping, scraping and the yelling of "bump!" We put down line quickly until dark, when we took a break, put our headlights on our helmets, and grabbed a bite of C-rats. Then we continued building line until we tied into a dozer line. It was late and the fire was laying down, so we were released to go to fire camp, where we were able to sleep for a few hours.

One of the best descriptions of a fire camp is in Michael Thoele's book *Fire Line: The Summer Battles of the West* (1995). Thoele calls the fire camp "an odd combination of Arab bazaar, D-Day beachhead, and class reunion." Take a fairly flat spot of ground some distance from the fire, throw in some large tents, possibly some trailers, billowing dust, a dining area that may or may not be covered with a tent, lots of noise from the generators – and add firefighters.

We crew members did not usually see all of the fire camp. Only our crew boss was allowed in the area where the plans and operations were determined. In this area were numerous tents to house the planning section, communications, first aid, finance, and check-in/demob (demobilization). We became familiar with the wash and toilet area, the tools area where we also picked up water and sack lunches, the dining area, and the sleeping area. Usually there was a bulletin board set up near the wash/kitchen area with information about the fire, news articles, and sometimes notes to individual firefighters.

On large fires, the camp would run nearly 24 hours a day.

The day crews started going through the dining area at 4:30 a.m., attended the strategy meeting or "morning briefing" near 6 a.m., then got the tools and lunches and water, jumped in the truck or helicopter and got to the fire before 8 a.m. The night crews were brought in, fed, and put to bed. Then the night crews were awakened, fed, briefed, and sent out to relieve the day crews. This cycle continued as long as necessary.

Companies were contracted to provide fire camp services, and after a while you got to recognize which caterer was on a fire. When we saw a red and white striped circus tent at fire camp, our taste buds perked up. The Black Hills catering service was known for its circus tent but even more for its great food. Other fire camps, particularly in California, used a crew of prison inmates to provide food service. On smaller fires, a local restaurant might put together meals, and someone would drive them out to us. When we were dog-tired and famished, food was food. We never complained, but there were noticeable differences in quality of meals.

After being awakened at 4:30 a.m., we splashed water on our faces and grabbed a quick breakfast of bacon, eggs, and pancakes, while our crew boss attended the morning briefing, providing the leaders of all of the day's resources a description of the plan of attack for the day. (Each leader is given a copy of the IAP, or incident action plan, which lists where each resource will be, along with a map of the fire, expected weather and fire behavior, radio frequencies in use, and who's in charge of different divisions on the fire.)

During these briefings, items of concern such as protection of watershed or archaeological values are noted, as well as the reiteration of any dangers or warnings for the day. Information provided by the night crew, such as areas of special concern, are discussed during the morning briefing. Once everyone gets to the assigned starting points, then we are briefed again for the specific task we are assigned, along with reiteration of any hazards for our assigned area.

Fighting a fire is like war – fire is the enemy and the

firefighter's job is to stop the advance. The firefighting operation is run like a battle, like a military operation. The fire is broken down into manageable units depending on the size of the fire. Divisions are created, usually a dividing up of the fire by geographical features such as a road, ridge top, or river. A qualified person is placed in charge of the division,(a division boss or division supe) who determines what is needed in the division to carry out the plan of attack. Divisions are further broken into sectors, with a sector boss in charge. Sectors can be further broken down into lines, with a line boss in charge of strategic sections of fireline. On huge fires, there may even be zones, which would encompass a group of divisions.

Resources are put together based on their qualifications and on the demands of the job. A remote area of the fire that requires hand crew work up against a hot fire will require hotshot crews (Type 1 crews), whereas mop-up work along a quiet piece of fireline can be handled by Type 2 crews – those not as experienced or well trained as the hotshots. Likewise, structure protection requires engine crews, with a mix of wildland engines providing outside defense and, when available, urban engines than can fight a structure fire. A fire boss is in charge of the entire operation, and has a series of subordinate bosses in charge of finances, logistics, and of course the fireline operations.

The design of this battle chart intends that no one person is directly responsible for more than ten people or resource units. As you can imagine, during the first stages of a wildfire, this ideal battle structure can be far from a smooth process. It can look like chaos for a while with initial attack forces handling numerous roles until enough people show up and spread the battle management among more personnel. As the fire grows, so does the organizational chart.

We got our marching orders for this second day on the fire. We loaded up into a helicopter and were flown to a different location along the edge of the fire. With the line construction work done yesterday and during the night, this fire was contained – so we were now tasked with mopping up. (This is dirty and brutal work, and for hotshot crews, it's the worst type of work. Once the fire has been contained, the effort becomes controlling the fire by either putting the fire out completely on small fires or by putting the fire out strategically on large fires. The object in mop-up is to cover a certain distance of burned ground from the fireline toward the interior of the fire area, making sure there are no hot spots left in the area.) Usually our crew was broken into pairs of two firefighters, one with a shovel and one with a Pulaski. Sometimes we were fortunate to have either a fire hose or a five-gallon bladder bag of water that we would wear like a backpack. Usually, though, we were a long, long way from any water.

We were to look for places on the ground where fire might be hiding, like in a stump hole or under a pile of unburned leaves, or beneath a pile of white ash. We would use the backs of our ungloved hands to feel over the tops of these places to sense any heat. If we did, we would dig and find the fire, then mix the burning debris with plain dirt until the debris was cool. With logs we had to chop out the burning section, then chop it up into small pieces and use dirt to extinguish and cool the pieces. Then we would take all the cooled pieces of burnt brush or trees and drag them into a burned, cleared area away from the fireline. This we called a bone pile, and the idea was if a hot ember was missed and the material started to burn, it was far enough away from the fireline to not be a threat.

After a day of this tedious work, we were covered head to toe with black and white ash mixed in with brown dust and caked with sweat. In fire camp, everyone could tell the hard-working crews by the volume of grime they were covered with. But if you worked your best at I,t you had the satisfaction of knowing that the area you worked on was no longer a worry and resources could be placed elsewhere. It was like your name and your reputation were staked to that area.

Finishing up a full day of mopping up, we arrived back at fire camp for a quick clean-up and dinner, then to the sleeping bags. The next morning we were up at 4:30 a.m., had a quick cleaning of the face and hands and a hot breakfast, and waited for our orders. This first fire we fought as a crew was called the Twin Rocks Fire, and was contained at 270 acres. Because the fire had been stopped and we had covered a good chunk of ground the day before in mop-up, we were released to go back to home base and clean up in preparation for the next fire. The hotshot crews were considered an initial attack resource, with quick mobility and the training for the toughest situations. Therefore it was common practice to release 'shot crews as quickly as possible so they could be available for another fire.

We arrived back at home base, and the crew members living in Santa Barbara were released to go home. The three of us living in the barracks replenished our gear and decided to hike into a well-known place called Red Rock, noted for skinny dipping. We were hoping to see some skin, but ended up stopping at a nice unoccupied swimming hole. The water looked so inviting that we jumped in and said the heck with looking for girls – for now. After some time jumping and splashing and enjoying the cool water, a couple of girls showed up, but in the company of their own guys. Soon the new arrivals were throwing off their swimsuits, while ours were still on. We decided it was time to leave, and we didn't get a chance to go back.

Our fellow firefighter from Compton, a young African American, wanted his hair trimmed one day, and I had the only vehicle among the three of us who lived in the barracks. Instead of asking me to take him 30 miles to a barber, he talked me into trimming his hair. Shoot, I had never trimmed hair before. His was an Afro style, all poofed out and quite popular in the late '60s and early '70s, and I was afraid to touch it for fear of messing it up. After he guaranteed he wouldn't kill me, I attacked his hair. Actually, except for one chunk I gouged out, it turned out okay. Thankfully, all I had to do was poof up his hair with his special hair fork, where I had gouged out a chunk. He never knew the difference. Besides, we wore hard hats most of the day anyway, so it really didn't matter. And, we were 30 miles from any teen-girl action, so what the heck.

A couple of days later, the Crew was working at the Ranger Station doing some hazard reduction, when I got a whiff of smoke. There were times when we considered the jobs we did while not fighting fires to be make-work activity, but work such as cutting down brush and making the ranger station safe from fire was necessary. It also kept us in shape. I yelled that I smelled smoke. We quit what we were doing and ran to the crew truck. One of the squad bosses had just started the truck when the siren blared once, meaning a fire down the canyon from the Ranger Station. The fire was less than a mile away in a draw separating the Ranger Station from the Forest Service government housing. We arrived at the edge of the draw and looked down the short but steep cliff to the fire below. We slid down the cliff and started building fireline. The Ranger District had all of the fire engines a few miles away on a training session, and once they arrived there was plenty of water. This fire, called the River Fire, was stopped at just an eighth of an acre, but it did get a couple of children into big trouble for playing with fireworks.

When not on a fire, we trained while working on various projects throughout the District. We had two separate sets of hand tools: our fireline tools and our training and project tools. We took special care of our fireline tools, keeping them painted, oiled, and sharpened. These were tools we would have to depend on, so we were very careful in maintaining the cutting edges. We sanded and treated the wooden handles, so they would stand up to heavy use on a fire. Our training and project tools were those we had used for a while on fires, tools that needed to be replaced. We kept these tools well maintained like our fireline tools, but they were too worn to rely on in a fire situation.

We learned how to tear apart, clean, and sharpen

chainsaws. They did a lot of cutting work for us, so we had to make sure they worked! Our training also included a section on working with portable fire pumps, for circumstances where that was an option. We had physical training in the mornings before we started work – warming up exercises and then a grueling run up and down a steep hill behind the compound. Occasionally we'd play a hard game of volleyball in the afternoon.

A week after that first fire, we loaded into the crew truck and headed to another fire on the District. It was only 9:35 a.m. Fires usually are quiet in the morning, so this didn't sound good. However, we had driven only a couple of miles, when we were told to return to base. Apparently the situation had been handled by local engine crews, so we were not needed.

The next day at just about quitting time, we were told to load up, and by 5:15 p.m. we were headed south for a fire that was threatening homes in the Saugus area outside of Los Angeles. We arrived just at dusk, so we had a quick view of the general area before darkness fell. While driving the dirt road behind the threatened subdivision, we passed a few fire engines and a Salvation Army station wagon with people handing out food. We were reminded of how hungry we were, but we kept driving into the hills and hoping the Salvation Army wagon would catch up with us. At last we came to the drop-off point, unloaded, grabbed our tools and web gear, turned on our headlamps, and marched off to the fireline. So much for dinner!

Engine crews were protecting the subdivision side of the fire, and a lot of the fire had been lined by dozers – except for one large area that was too rugged for dozers. Our task was to build fireline throughout the night, burn out to strengthen the fireline, then hold it. We'd build a length of fireline, then one of the squad bosses would start burning along the fire side of our line. (Usually the squad bosses carried a half dozen or so fusees that were perfect for starting fires without matches). Line building was a little faster using this method because we could cut down a little on the width of the fireline and use the blackened area we burned as part of the fireline width. So all night we built line and burned. Sometimes we had to yell for a shovel to throw dirt onto a large clump of brush flaming up and threatening to spread across the fireline. By morning light we were tired, but we had completed the fireline into a box canyon.

Waiting to be relieved, we spread out along the fireline mopping up and patrolling to make sure no fire threatened the line. Our worst area was the box canyon, with our line into the narrow canyon keeping the fire from jumping to the other side. I was near to the last crew member in the canyon, and it was a scary situation. As the morning progressed, the day's heat started rising while the humidity started dropping. The fire was starting to pick up in places.

We were expecting to be pulled from the fireline by now, and we were hungry and tired. Luckily, a few of us had cans of crackers or pecan cake roll tucked away in our web gear for just such an occasion – but that's not dinner or breakfast, and we had missed both. The atmosphere in that canyon was charged with a tired panic, and given the right words, we would have abandoned our patrol areas with vigor. However, we avoided the panic and continued to patrol while waiting for the word to leave. Finally, at 12:15 p.m. we were relieved of line duty. As we were hiking out of the area, looking back, I saw a bulldozer working on the ridge above the box canyon we had just left. Seemed like a waste of our effort, but I guess we bought some time for the building of a stronger fireline on that ridge. After cleaning up at camp, eating, and grabbing a paper sleeping bag, we slept.

A paper sleeping bag was fairly common on fires back then – layers and layers of soft brown kraft paper were formed into a sleeping bag seamed on three sides with an opening at the top. It was more comfortable than sleeping on the bare ground, but not by much. They were handy for the camp crew during cleanup – you just tossed them into a fire when you were done with them.

We woke up for dinner, and were preparing for another night on the fireline when the crew boss told us we were to stay in camp and get some more rest. No one argued, and we got a better sleep that night. The next morning was a typical early wake-up but this day our assignment was to demob. Demob, or demobilization, is the releasing of crews, equipment or other resources back to their home base. The crew boss has to handle paperwork including time sheets, get it all signed and submitted to the finance section with the incident management team, while the crew cleans up the sleeping area. Broken or lost tools or equipment are replaced at the camp's tool cache.

When it was all wrapped up we headed home from the San Fran Fire, which had been stopped at 4,280 acres. On the way back to Santa Barbara, we stopped off for lunch at the city of Filmore, where we found an A&W. We just about cleared the place out, not only thanks to our odor, but we also looked like a bunch of prison convicts. We were dressed in our travel clothes from our war bags, sort-of-clean blue jeans and khaki long-sleeve shirts, and riding in a crew truck with an emblem on the side that no one recognized. Plus, wherever we went, we walked in single file, like an army platoon, or like a crew of prisoners. Once we explained that we weren't prisoners, we enjoyed a lunch and shared some fire stories with a few people interested in what we did.

On the way home, traveling U.S. Highway 101 through Santa Barbara, we had a convertible pull up alongside. Those on the driver's side of our truck looked down and then the whole crew moved over to the driver's side. All 14 of the crew were hanging out the side, eyes wide, voices yelling encouragement and looking down onto the young lady driver as she unbuttoned her blouse, giving us quite a show. That sure rejuvenated us, even though she probably thought we were prisoners! This happened to us a couple of more times while traveling on the highway. Aaaah, summertime in Southern California!

We got back to home base that afternoon, and spent the

rest of the day cleaning and sharpening tools and chainsaws, cleaning up the crew truck, and replenishing the food and water. That evening the crew was called to a fire out of Monterey.

During the working day, a fire call response was immediate. But, during off hours, we had to be in the crew truck and on the road to the fire within two hours. So, the three of us staying in the barracks had the advantage of getting ready without the hurry, and we had the crew stuff ready by the time the rest of the guys arrived.

With the entire crew in the truck, we were heading north on Highway 154 toward Monterey when the crew boss got a call and was told to return to base. Apparently the local fire attack in Monterey was able to take care of the fire without our help, so we turned around and headed home.

It was now the week of July 4th, and everyone in fire operations were biting their nails and sniffing the air, worried about fires started by people – and especially children playing with fireworks. We lucked out, as the few fires caused by fireworks in the area were all kept small.

The day after Independence Day, however, we got an afternoon fire call to go to the Monterey area for a fire not far from Big Sur country. This area along the California coast south of San Francisco became a famous hangout for writers and painters in the '50s and early '60s, then became popular with the hippie movement of the late '60s and early '70s. The Santa Lucia mountains rise up very quickly from the Pacific Ocean, in places going from sea level to nearly 5,000 feet elevation in only three miles.

We arrived in the area near dusk, and immediately ran into an access problem. A lowboy truck hauling a dozer into the fire area had slipped its rear wheels off a sharp curve, and the rear deck was hanging over a dropoff into a small but intimidating draw – and of course the alignment of this wreck blocked all traffic into the fire. We grabbed our tools and gear and hiked to the fire, wondering how the dozer was going to get safely off-loaded so the road could be opened. We all said the same thing, "Glad we weren't driving."

Upon arrival at the fire, we were assigned to build fireline in a mixed pine and brush area. As we moved along building line, we stumbled upon a few local residents working in their own fashion. We chuckled to ourselves – here we were in fire-resistant clothes, long sleeves, hard hats, heavy boots, fire shelters hanging from our web gear, and leather gloves; these locals were barefoot, short-sleeved or no shirt at all, bareheaded and bare-handed. We joked that they were out there trying to protect their hidden marijuana crop.

After an all-night operation of building line, we were relieved. We spent the day sleeping in fire camp as best we could. We were awakened, fed, and out on the fireline just before dark that second night. Since the fire was contained and quiet, we just mopped up all night. When morning came we were again relieved and spent another day in camp. Late in the afternoon we were told to load up and head back to home base. So we left the Skinner Ridge Fire, which was stopped at 90 acres.

The trip home was an adventure to say the least. After leaving the fire camp, our crew boss asked which of us had been on the famous Pacific Coast Highway. Only a few of us had. So instead of taking Highway 101 back, we took the scenic route home, along the famous Highway 1. It was dusk, and traffic at this time of evening was extremely light. Along a deserted stretch of highway, a small car drove up and then alongside the crew truck in an attempt to pass. One of us was always on the lookout for girls driving by, and as the car approached the lookout yelled to check out the scenery in the car.

One of the crew members, priding himself on his charm and charisma, had us hold his feet with his head extended into the passenger window of the girls' car. Luckily, it was dusk, and we could see car headlights quite a ways ahead. So, a couple of us played lookout watching for lights, while our Casanova visited with the girls. After he shared a few quick kisses with the passenger girl, we hauled him back into the truck before the next curve. The young lady driving the car had to be commended for keeping it close enough to the truck, so we could pull off the stunt.

A week later, during the mid-afternoon, the fire alarm blared. We loaded up and headed toward Highway 154. The fire was on the coast side of San Marcos Pass. When we reached the top of the pass, we headed out on the West Camino Cielo, the ridge on top of the Santa Ynez Mountains. We all thought this could be another Coyote or Refugio Fire. We didn't want that happening on our watch, so we jumped into the line building with gusto.

I happened to be working on a small ridge as lead brush hook, and I spied a B-17 airtanker flying up from the Goleta air attack base. From our location we could look down and almost see the aircraft taking off from the base. The B-17 had four engines, and was huge compared with most of the aircraft we usually saw working a fire. After a couple of more chops with my brush hook into the 10-foot tall brush, I glanced up and found myself looking right into the eyes of the B-17 pilot. I yelled "Drop!" and we all hit the ground face down.

We'd been warned about the dangers of being hit directly by a load of fire retardant. In the past, when bentonite was mixed with water for retardant, the mix would sometimes contain chunks of material that had not been mixed very well. And when the doors opened and gallons of the retardant fell from a speeding plane, these chunks were known to have injured firefighters and smashed vehicles. Though the retardant now was less prone to being lumpy, we still were taught to drop to the ground if you couldn't get away from the drop zone.

I am sure the pilot, with a giggle, told the co-pilot, "Watch this." And, damn, if he didn't dump the retardant right on us! After he passed overhead, we stood up trying to shake off the pink retardant – we must have looked like a bunch of wet dogs shaking off water. I grabbed my pink brush hook and with the first swing, it went sailing into the tall brush in front of me. After a few choice words, I warned the rest of the crew to be careful, that the handles were really slick. I crawled into the brush and retrieved the hook and rubbed enough mud and dirt over the handle to keep a grip on it.

Later that night after the sun had been down for a while, we were finally able to take a dinner break. We sat in a shallow cave, more like a rock overhang, shivering and shaking, trying to eat our C-rats. Even though it was hours ago that we had been dumped on, we were still wet from the retardant. Where it had stuck to our skin, it was flaking off, but the clothes were a different matter. My white underclothes were now pink and still wet.

We cussed that pilot, but we also thanked him – his drops had helped stop the fire at only 16 acres. After a few hours of sleep, we went back to the fire, called the Indian Caves Fire, and spent the day mopping up. It was one of those strange coincidences that we used the old fireline from the Refugio Fire of 1955 to stop the westward advance of this fire.

Another week went by, with us doing hazard reduction work around the Station complex and keeping in shape with running and exercises. There was a fairly good hill climb adjacent to our station, and the game was to run the hill and beat the clock. We were on guard for rattlesnakes and yellow jacket hornets; we often got stung, but no one was snake bitten. While working around the family housing at the Station one day, one of the crew members had a yellow jacket hornet get inside his pants. Under the circumstances, he still behaved as a gentleman, holding in the four-letter words and keeping his pants on. We rushed him to our crew truck where he could remove his pants out of sight of the families and deal with the crisis.

Another task to keep us in shape was working on fuel breaks. Ever since the catastrophic fires of 1955 and 1964, a series of fuel breaks were built along the ridge tops to break up the continuity of fuels. The theory was to cut a swath from a huge patch of brush, then plant grass in the opening. Although the grass would burn, it provided both a temporary reprieve from the tremendous heat of the burning brush as well a place where a fireline could quickly be built.

Some of the first fuel breaks were built using a length of surplus anchor chain tied between two dozers. We got to see some of this anchor chain, stored in the boneyard at the Station, and it was huge! The idea was to hook the anchor chain in between two bulldozers, and in dragging it, the brush was ripped and pulverized. It was a little too effective, though, it chewed up the ground much more than planned. So, it was back to hand work for the crew. Because we were working on ridge tops, and the Santa Ynez Mountains were mostly sandstone with lots of boulders, we'd stage boulder-rolling contests on our breaks. We had to discontinue our fun after a few days, when we nearly smashed a passing vehicle on the dirt road below us.

It had been a week since our last fire, when we received a call to load up and head south to the Mt. Pinos area. Once again, we made it a few miles before we were told to return to station.

The next evening at about 10:30 p.m., we were told to load up and head south. Our destination this time was out of Kernville, in central California. It took most of the night to get to the fire, and during this night drive I encountered my first claustrophobic person. To cut the chill of the night air while driving through the desert to Kernville, we rolled down the canvas sides of the crew truck. I was sitting at the very tail end of the truck near the steps at the opening of the canvas cover, and one of our crew members woke up and suddenly lurched at the doorway. He was wild-eyed and looking like he would jump out of the truck. Luckily, a couple of the football players sitting near me joined in, and we calmed him down.

We stopped to get breakfast along the way, and arrived at the fire camp early in the morning. We were loaded into helicopters and dropped off on the far side of the fire, where we started building line by 11 a.m. Line construction went fairly quickly in this juniper/brush and grass environment, and we were relieved around 5:30 p.m. after tying in the firelines. I had to replace my brush hook when we arrived back in camp, because after chopping the extra hard manzanita the blade had started chipping. We were sent out again the next day to mop up and improve the firelines. This fire was called the James Fire, and it was contained at 1,400 acres.

A couple of days later, we had two fire calls in the middle of the night. The first one was for Monterey. We were heading north on Highway 154, when we were turned around and sent back to Santa Barbara for a fire in Rattlesnake Canyon. Local firefighters were able to stop these two fires, though, so we were sent back home.

On July 30, at 5 p.m., we were sent south for a fire out of San Diego. It was still daylight while driving through the metro Los Angeles area, and I happened to be riding with the crew boss in the chase truck instead of in the crew truck. Along one stretch of eight-lane freeway, we noticed a vehicle pull off to the right side of the freeway; the driver got out of the car and threw something at the crew truck. We kept our eye on this guy wondering what he was trying to do. When he stopped for the second time and again threw something at the crew truck, the crew boss pulled over and went to speak with the guy. Turns out he thought the crew truck was carrying a load of convicts, so he was trying to throw them packs of cigarettes.

About seven hours later we arrived at the Ranger Station near the fire on the Cleveland National Forest. We grabbed a little sleep before getting a quick breakfast. We started working on the Guata Fire first thing in the morning, cutting fireline to keep this brush-fed fire from growing and threatening the scattered homes in the area. The fire was not far from the highway, and not very many miles from the Mexico border.

During the day we noticed the red and white fire engines of the California Division of Forestry heading southeast on the highway past our fire without stopping. Soon we spotted a large column of smoke to the southeast, and we heard there was a fire burning in Mexico and threatening to cross the border. We figured we would head that way soon, but we were kept on this 70-acre fire. The next day we went back into the fire to mop up, and we were demobed that night and drove home.

We were complaining of having to drive all that way for just a small fire. But, the overhead people knew something we didn't. We were just in the beginning of the disaster season. Two months later, the area we had worked in burned over in the catastrophic Laguna Fire which killed eight people, destroyed nearly 400 homes, and burned over 175,000 acres.

Living in the barracks definitely had its advantages. We had arrived at the station at 5:30 a.m., and those who lived in Santa Barbara headed home to clean up and rest. The three of us in the barracks cleaned our clothes, ate, and rested. At 2 p.m. we got a call to head to Santa Maria. When the rest of the crew arrived, we headed north in the heat of the afternoon. The fire was in the Cuyama Valley northeast of Santa Maria. While driving a straight stretch in the valley with the smoke column visible in the distance, our crew truck decided to give up the ghost and die. So here we were alongside the highway, with steam and smoke coming from our truck, and the smoke column of the fire we are supposed to be fighting off in the distance. After putting out the fire in the engine compartment, we waited for a good hour until a school bus, quickly leased by the Forest Service, arrived to take us to the Cowhead Fire. We spent the night working on the firelines, and the fire was stopped at 150 acres.

We arrived back at the Station that evening just in time to turn around and head out again. The fire was in a remote area called the Sespe Condor Sanctuary, one of two sanctuaries set aside for the protection of the California Condor. While it was still dark early in the morning, we started building fireline at the base of the hill on which the fire was burning. About noon, my squad was detailed to load into a helicopter and work the top of this hill. The object, we were told, was to pinch the fire into this narrow canyon, which was supposed to be rocky and very lightly fueled. We were to build fireline on top. Sounded reasonable, but our crew boss expressed his reservations. He was overruled by the fire boss, so we were helicoptered to the top of the ridge.

As we were waiting for the last crew member to come in, we grabbed a quick bite to eat and one of the crew members went around the hill into the brush to relieve himself. We heard a roar like a fast freight train and then a yell. The crew member came ripping out of the brush pulling up his pants and yelling with the fire right behind him. We were up in seconds, but we were quickly surrounded by thousands of burning brands. Our last crew member, Baltimore, was still in the helicopter. There was no place to land on our hilltop now – it was being overrun by fire. Instead of taking Baltimore back down to join the other squad, the Vietnam-veteran pilot hovered against the backside of our hill and told Baltimore to get out. In the panic, Baltimore jumped out of the helicopter the wrong way while the pilot was trying to get his aircraft away from the blowup. A guardian angel was with Baltimore, for he missed running into the helicopter blades by just inches.

We were being bombarded with burning embers and yellow jacket hornets. We weren't sure which was worse – the burns or the stings. We were surrounded by fires started by more burning embers than we could handle, so we had to abandon the hill and move to a safer area.

We backed off to the next ridge, a short walk from our lost firefight, and were able to watch the rest of our crew work up a ridge across a steep draw from us, following the edge of the fire.

We had just jumped out of a bad situation, only to see the rest of our crew work themselves into another bad situation. The fire had spotted into the canyon below the crew. While a couple members of the crew were carefully working down to the spot fire, it decided to grow with a vengeance, nearly trapping the crew. Later that evening, we caught up with each other and tied in that section of line, and shared stories of the too-close-for-comfort situations we had just come through.

Figuring on a night without food under the stars, we heard a helicopter coming up the canyon. Amazed – as fire support helicopters did not fly after dusk – we watched as the helicopter dropped a load of cargo in the clearing near us. We opened the metal milk cans in the cargo net and found hot steaks, potatoes, and fixings for breakfast along with fresh water and other beverages. Perhaps this manna from heaven was a peace offering for nearly getting the crew killed.

After a night of sleeping on the ground, we woke up early to eat and started working on the line. Our goal was to finish a very steep section of fireline and tie into a line created by smokejumpers the day before. This steep slope, the back side of the ridge we'd lost the day before, created some problems for us. The fire was above in trees, and logs and the burning material was ready to roll down the hill. We decided that a deep, wide trench was needed to hold this hillside and keep the rolling debris from running down the unburned hillside.

The two of us shorties on the crew were tasked with keeping the rolling debris from hurting the crew members who were digging the deep trench along the side hill. The two of us walked back and forth across the hillside turning logs so they wouldn't roll and trenching the logs that we couldn't turn. A photographer happened by and took our photos as we were working this area – said he was doing a story for the *National Geographic*, but I have never seen this story or any of the photographs.

As the line was progressing through this steep area, a part of a burning log broke free and started rolling downhill. Baltimore was the closest to this rolling log and immediately took off after it; however, he lost his balance on the steep slope and rolled after the burning log. I gave chase along with a couple other crew members, but Baltimore yelled up from the bottom saying he was fine and that he could handle the burning log.

We tied in with the smokejumper line and worked on

reinforcing it. We went to sleep on the fireline with C-rats for dinner and taking turns as lookout. The next morning the helicopter picked us up and off-loaded us at the fire camp where we cleaned up, ate, and rested.

'Baltimore' had a fear of the convicts who often worked in fire camp on the larger fires in California – perhaps it was the growling attitude of one of the kitchen crew when I asked for scrambled eggs that morning. The prison inmate serving the eggs looked at me, said "So you want them scrambled huh?" and proceeded to chop and beat the hell out of three eggs on the griddle with his pancake flipper.

For whatever reason, John from Baltimore was too scared to go use the porta-potty since the prison inmates were lounging around the area. After watching his agony, we finally talked him into using the porta-potty and told him a couple of us crewmembers would be standing by. Two of the guys snuck up to the porta-potty while 'Baltimore' was in there and started rocking the toilet. Unfortunately in their exuberance, they tilted it too far and it crashed onto its side. Poor Baltimore rolled out the door, jumped up, hiked up his pants and scooted away from the convicts, whom he thought had done the dirty deed.

The Poplar Fire was stopped at 1310 acres. We were demobed at lunch time and headed home.

As we were driving the narrow dirt road out of the Sespe Condor Sanctuary, we spied a couple of female sunbathers on a beach along Sespe Creek. It was rare to see that much water flowing in the creek, but our attention was riveted on the sunbathers. We had to stop the crew bus and check out the beach. Probably scared the girls to death, as nearly a dozen grubby, stinky guys came out of the bus heading for them. But, the girls soon figured out that the horny guys were just saying hi and trying to get a peek. After a short visit and goodbyes, we loaded up and kept the bus pointed toward home.

As with most fires in Southern California, this one had been started by someone, not by Mother Nature. We heard later that it was an accidental fire caused by a famous country musician who had driven across some parched grass to get to a fishing hole, and the hot exhaust set the grass on fire.

Things calmed down during the next two weeks, with only two fire calls in which we were returned to the Station while en route. I had to quit early to get ready for college, and so I missed the rest of the fire season.

A few weeks after I left all hell broke loose throughout California. Numerous fires broke out, hammering the firefighting resources of California. The year 1970 became known as the California Disaster Season. I found out years later that the ICS, or Incident Command System, that is used today for managing firefighting efforts and resources was a result of reviewing the disastrous 1970 California fire season.

Interregional Fire Crew

There was still no word regarding the fire blowing up in the Salmon River Canyon, but I was able to use the restless wait to advantage – I finished one of the computers and started work on the second one. I always carry two fire bags in my car: one with structure firefighting gear and the other with wildfire gear. Both bags were checked and rechecked, ready to go. I was ready for either working on a wildfire situation or changing into the heavier structure protective gear if we had to work on house fires. While scanning the second computer for virus issues, my mind wandered back to when I was in college.

After graduating from Santa Barbara City College in 1971, with a two-year associate degree, I headed up to Montana, to settle in Missoula where the University of Montana's School of Forestry had accepted me as a student. With the help of my advisor, I lined out a regimen of courses for a bachelor's in forestry, with an emphasis in fire management. Since I had taken most of the core courses at Santa Barbara, I could concentrate on just the forestry courses at Missoula.

One day in one of my fire science classes, the professor asked each of us to provide our fire experience. After class one of the other students walked up and asked if I wanted a summer job. He seemed impressed that I had been on the Los Prietos Hotshots and said he wanted me on his crew. He had recently toured out of the Marines and had taken on the job of superintendent for the Bitterroot Interregional Fire Crew. Sounded good to me. The paperwork was a formality, and I was on the crew.

As a struggling college student, I still couldn't afford a pair of White's boots, and I was not going to purchase a cheap pair like the Red Wings again. I did find a pair of Buffalos on sale, and after I had them re-soled with a heavy Vibram sole, I was booted up for a hundred dollars less than the White's. After school was out, I loaded up my clothes, new boots, and bicycle and drove the two hours south of Missoula to the community of Sula for the summer of 1972.

The Bitterroot Interregional Fire Crew was created in 1963 and was part of a nine-crew highly mobile and trained cadre of firefighters ready to travel anywhere in the United States. This aspect of mobility was a little different from the hotshot crews, which generally stayed within the Region they were assigned to. By 1972, the number of Interregional Fire Crews had increased to nineteen.

The work center for the Bitterroot IR crew was 15 miles off Highway 93 east of Sula. The road followed the East Fork of the Bitterroot River, with places of dense lodgepole pine on one side of the road and the river on the other side. Our camp was near the boundary of the Anaconda-Pintler Wilderness. We had a beautiful location, with cabins for sleeping all of the crew, the superintendent and his family, and the cook, a bathroom and showers cabin, a cabin with a pool table and a ping-pong table, and a mess hall. A small creek ran through the facility, and we would sometimes catch trout there. It was great to not have to cook our meals during the work days, since we had a cook providing two meals a day plus sack lunches, five days a week. Sula consisted of a bar, a grocery store/gas station/post office, a few scattered homes, and numerous small mom-and-pop sawmills. It had the distinction of being the last community in southwest Montana if you were headed south on Highway 93 into Idaho.

The Rocky Knob bar was a popular hangout for the crew on the rare occasions that we went into Sula on a day off. A special drink named after the crew consisted of a dangerous mix of alcohols generously sprinkled with black pepper. The object was to gulp this concoction as soon as the pepper was added and before the bubbling stopped. You weren't part of the crew until you had been through this ceremony! Needless to say I did my duty, but thank heavens we had to do it only once.

The bar had a great pool table, but it also had low windows in the pool room. We paid for a window or two, even though we tried to keep the balls on the table. One day, on a day off, I figured on riding my bicycle to Sula and back, a 30-mile round trip. A few miles from Sula I had stopped to take a break, when I heard and then saw movement in the brush along the creek. A bull moose popped out of the brush, surprising us both. I froze, as I could tell he wasn't pleased with the human smell in his territory. After a few feints at running toward me – and me not moving a twitch – he finally ambled off. After a renewed stint of breathing I continued on pedaling to Sula.

Physical fitness for a fire crew is paramount, and we ran every morning. It was a two-mile flat-out gut wrencher, because we had to beat the ex-Marine superintendent or run it again. This guy was in his 30's and in good shape. We started on June 18 and immediately stepped into the regulated training to create a crew that can handle the toughest situations and survive.

After the classroom training, we put the line building skills to work and were tasked with building fire breaks in creeks and in areas along logging operations in preparation for fall burning. We practiced the same style line building that we had done on the Los Prietos Hotshots, and we kept two sets of tools: one for fire and one for project work.

On some days, we would arrive back at the station early from a day working on fire breaks and finish up our day with a hard, no-rules volleyball game. It was rough and tumble, and we had to wear our boots. But we were expressly forbidden to get hurt, because we were needed on the crew.

This crew had a real bus, not a flatbed canvas-covered truck. The bus had a rear area fenced off so that tools could be safely hauled with us. Gas and oil for the chainsaws was carried in an outside compartment. It was quickly determined that because I did not like the taste of beer, I would be one of the three bus drivers.

The fire season for the Bitterroot IR crew started slow, and we didn't get our first fire call until July 8. We were all excited; we were sick and tired of working in creeks cutting fireline around logged areas. The call came in at 7:30 p.m., so we ran out to the bus, loaded up, and started down the dirt road toward Highway 93. As soon as we hit the highway, we were turned back – but four days later we got a call to head to New Mexico. We hot-rodded up to Missoula.

Montana in those days had no speed limit during the day, and a 75 mph speed limit for trucks at night. Missoula was the closest airport. It housed the smokejumper base as well as the offices of Johnson Flying Service, who had been providing air transport services to the Forest Service since the 1930's. There were two Interregional Fire Crews using the Missoula airport for flying out to a fire: our crew and the Lolo IR Fire Crew. When dispatched, we had a two-hour response time to get to the airport and be ready to board, or we would be left behind and the crew given a bad name. From our base near the Anaconda-Pintler to the Missoula airport was 90 miles, with 15 miles of dirt road, and we had to slow down for the towns of Conner, Darby, Hamilton, and Missoula. Now the Lolo IR Crew, our rival, was based to the west of Missoula near the Plains area. They had a little less distance to travel and over better roads, but the object for us was to beat the Lolo IR to the airport and load first. We did every time – I'm sure we could have won any bus drag races in those days!

The Bitterroot IR Crew of 1972 had a very tough situation ahead of it. The ex-Marine superintendent was tasked with producing a completely new crew, after the previous Bitterroot crew had been disbanded for drugs and alcohol. The reputation of the Bitterroot IR was at rock bottom. So the little rivalry concerning the first to the airport was a small effort in the big picture of change and respectability. We had to work harder and play harder than any of the other crews.

This need to exceed, to build back the crew respectability, nearly killed us. But, we did survive, and we did move the crew out of the cellar of respectability.

We were assigned to the Little Moccasin Fire, in Mesa Verde National Park in the Southwest's Four Corners area west of Durango, Colorado. This first fire of the season for the crew gave us an idea of what we could be in for the rest of the season: we had to escape into the black three times that first afternoon while trying to go head to head against a hot fire. After a couple of days building line and a half day of mop-up, we were called off the line and told to head back to Boise for a different fire. We quickly changed after a fast cleanup, and waved goodbye to the 2,800-acre Little Moccasin.

It was interesting to note that this Little Mocassin fire became a turning point in the concern over the protection of antiquities. Even though we had been given "the lecture" regarding the antiquities, somehow other resources on the fire had apparently missed those talks!

Mesa Verde National Park (July 1972)

A lightning-caused fire burned 2,680 acres in Mesa Verde National Park and on Ute Mountain Tribal lands. The Park failed to recognize the potential for cultural resource damage from fire suppression activities, and the work (primarily dozers) resulted in the destruction of numerous archeological sites. A post-fire review and investigation prompted the establishment of a national policy to include cultural resource oversight in the management of wildland fires on all federal lands (from NPS Fire History Timeline).

Years later on the Poe Cabin Fire, I witnessed this change in dealing with antiquities. A member of the fire management team was appointed as cultural resource officer and was in charge of ensuring that artifact sites were protected as well as possible during suppression activities. Because the Poe Cabin

Fire was burning on ground once frequented by the Nez Perce Indians, there was a definite concern over the preservation of pictographs and possible burial sites in the area.

From Mesa Verde National Park, we bussed to Farmington and loaded up into a Johnson Air DC-3 for the flight to Boise. This DC-3 had facing benches instead of seats, and as soon as the plane left the ground, I was lying on the floor so I wouldn't get air sick. The fire situation had calmed down by the time we arrived in Boise, so we ended up spending the rest of the day and one night on standby in the old military barracks of Gowen Field in Boise.

During our stay, we were able to tour the BIFC, or Boise Interagency Fire Center (now called NIFC, the National Interagency Fire Center), which was the control center responsible for equipping and overseeing firefighting efforts throughout the United States. It was interesting to see how the system worked and to meet some of the people responsible for moving thousands of firefighters and tons of supplies and equipment all over the United States. The next day we were released to fly back to Missoula.

During the 1972 fire season, the Bitterroot IR crew was chosen (or volunteered by our superintendent) for testing of physical fitness and work capacity conditions during a firefighting operation. (For a few years, the Forest Service had been using what's called the step test, in which you step up and down on a step at the cadence of a metronome. Your heart rate is checked before and after, and a value is determined from the results. The higher the number, the better shape you are in.) Researchers were examining how well the step test related to the actual physical demands of firefighting work, and our crew were test subjects.

One member of the crew was trained to take the required heart rate readings. He was tasked with measuring not only heart rates but also weather conditions and temperatures. Called the mule, he carried the chainsaw gas, the weather kit, the first aid kit, and the testing materials and documents. He would help as a swamper, dragging cut brush and trees away from the chainsaws in between stopping and taking people's pulse rates.

Each day on a fire, one crew member was selected to be the test subject. During a long and hard fire fight, we would nearly plead to be the test subject because that meant more breaks during the day. The data from this project was used to re-evaluate the step test, and eventually led to its being replaced by the currently used pack test.

Three days after our return from Boise, we were called out to a fire in Utah. Once again, we raced Lolo IR to get to the airport first and razzed them when they showed up behind us. After stopping at the Spokane airport for two more crews, and fueling the plane, we flew to Cedar City, Utah. From thousands of feet above the fire, we could see a bunch of red glowing spots against the dark black of the night. After landing, we stopped for breakfast, then bussed to Beaver. We unloaded our war bags and hopped into a truck to take us to a spot fire that the incident commander was worried about. One of those hurry-up-and-wait deals, we unloaded in a nice meadow along the road and watched the spot fire while waited for orders.

We got worried as the morning warmed up – we should have been on that spot fire at first light while it was quiet and cool. We were finally sent to help line the spot fire, while the other crews tackled the main fire.

I was one of four sent to scout between the main fire and the spot fire, making sure we didn't have more spot fires in between. Things started heating up. Pretty soon what sounded like a freight train could be heard, but we couldn't see it because of the trees. It quickly turned ugly as both fires blew up, with the four of us in the middle. Everybody was told to bug out, to get back to the meadow, which was our safety zone. Scrambling through the dense trees, wondering if we were going to make it out alive, we were able to find our way out and back to the meadow, catching up with the rest of the crew.

For the next five days, we either trucked in or flew in by helicopter to mop up. After six days on this 1,400-acre fire called Sheeprock, we were finally released and got home on July 27.

During this fire, I had my nice government-issued sleeping bag stolen. Damn, we had never experienced or heard of stealing on a fire before. I learned how tiresome it was to try to deal with government employees in two different regions trying to get a replacement sleeping bag. After that, we took better steps to protect our gear.

We had been back at Sula just a day when we were called to a fire out of Salmon, Idaho. This area was within driving distance for us. So, we loaded up and drove the bus to the fire camp at Corn Creek on the Salmon River.

Corn Creek is a campground situated at the end of the North Fork road which is the upstream beginnings of the famous River of No Return. The River of No Return is so named because of the extreme difficulty in getting back up the river. Thanks to modern jet boats which have the power to navigate whitewater rapids, travel up and down the Salmon River is not nearly so difficult as in the past. But, it's no less treacherous for boaters unfamiliar with the river.

In the morning after breakfast, we loaded up in the helicopter and were flown to the top of the ridge overlooking the fire. The plan was to build a fireline down the steep ridge to the river. We slid down the ridge building fireline, and when we came to the river, a jet boat would take us across the river. We would climb back into the helicopter and head back up to the top of the ridge. The jet boat was the highlight of the fire; I'd never been on one.

On our next slide down a different ridge, punching in a quick line to the river, a second crew above us was improving the fast line. It was late in the afternoon, and everyone was getting tired. The fire got away from the crew above us, and headed up the hill. The incident commander called our superintendent and offered a keg of beer if we could catch the fire. Climbing up the steep slope, we caught the fire, and turned it over to the crew behind us. The we continued down the ridge building line.

We were so tired that we could barely lift one foot after the other. One of the squad bosses got hit in the head, just below the hard hat, with a small rock that had been dislodged. Normally, that would have been shrugged off with an ouch and a few four-letter words. But as tired as we were, it sent him falling and then rolling down the steep hillside. Of course, this had to have happened to the largest guy on our crew. I was the nearest one below him, and heard the commotion. I braced to catch him, and the next nearest crewmember rushed up to help me. We stopped him from rolling any farther. The crew superintendent radioed the division boss alerting him of the situation.

We didn't have EMTs on the crew in those days, but the "mule" carried a first aid kit that would do for lesser type injuries. The division boss notified the fire camp of the emergency, and the first aid people at the fire camp fixed up a Stokes litter with some first aid supplies. A helicopter was tasked to bring the Stokes to us. The rocky slope we were on prevented the helicopter from bringing anyone to help – and it couldn't pick up the injured squad boss. So, the pilot had to carefully maneuver the Stokes that was dangling by long line below the helicopter to a spot in the rocks where he could release the line. We loaded the squad boss into the Stokes and manhandled him through a large boulder-strewn rock slide down to a jet boat waiting at the water's edge. Once we'd loaded the Stokes into the jet boat, the squad boss was taken across the river to a waiting ambulance, and then driven to the nearest hospital in Salmon, Idaho. The squad boss spent a night in the hospital, and was released the next day with just a few bruises and minor cuts.

The next day, we spent mopping up part of the fire with the help of a helicopter dropping bucket loads of water. During the heat of the afternoon, we quickly learned to call in a water drop on a hot spot then step into the path of the bucket drop. It was a great way to cool off, but we had to be careful. We would watch the water being released from the overhead bucket. Then we would move to get into the mist of the water drop rather than taking a direct hit.

We were released to go home that evening from the Butte Creek Fire, which was stopped at 90 acres. But on the way, with the thanks of the incident commander, a keg of beer was waiting at the Northfork tavern. The celebration was on, not only celebrating the successful end of the fire, but also the return of the squad boss. I had to drive the bus home full of fellow crew members all feeling no pain.

Two days later, we were back in the Salmon country helping the North Fork District with numerous lightning fires. We were assigned to the Indianola Guard Station, where we were broken into two- and three-person teams that were then flown in to the fires by helicopter.

The fire I was on was quickly put down, and we left it completely cold. At dark, we hiked out to the nearest road and waited until we got a ride back to the Guard Station. By late that night, all of us were back at the station, and the crew was released to drive home.

While waiting for the next fire, we spent some time boning up on chainsaw skills by working in a large snag patch in the Sleeping Child drainage. This particular area of the Bitterroot National Forest was comprised of thousands of snags, standing trees that had burned and died.

In one of my fire science classes at the University of Montana, we studied the Sleeping Child Fire of 1961, which burned 27,900 acres of lodgepole pine. The fire was lightning-caused, hitting an area of lodgepole that had been dead or dying since the mountain pine beetle outbreak during the 1930's. The downed trees provided tons of burnable fuel, and on August 4, 1961, the weather conditions were just right for a fast, intense fire.

We were in the same area eleven years later working in one of the huge snag patches, leaving a few wildlife trees, but getting the rest of the snags down on the ground. There was concern that, because the regeneration of much of this burned area was coming in very heavy, (in some places there were tens of thousands of seedlings per acre,) having many standing snags could be like a lightning rods attracting lightning to the regenerating stand.

After four days of this, we were awakened just after midnight to go to McCall, Idaho. We raced to Missoula, then flew to McCall, where we ate breakfast at the smokejumper loft. We bussed to the old mining town of Warren, where we transferred into smaller trucks. We headed down the narrow winding road to the small fire camp set up at the South Fork Guard Station, on the South Fork of the Salmon River. From there, we were driven to the fire in Pony Creek, where we started building fireline. The area was steep and rugged. We had heard that a couple of smokejumpers had been injured on the jump into this fire. We could still see a chute or two on the hillside.

In the early afternoon, half of the crew got very sick, including me, and we were trucked back to the fire camp. The next day, those of us sick were left in camp to rest, while the rest of the crew worked on mop-up. That evening, we were released to head home, leaving the Pony Creek Fire at 100 acres. After a couple of days of rest, all of us who had been sick were feeling better, and started back into the daily grind.

On August 10, we were called out to a fire on the Bitterroot National Forest, near Hamilton. We arrived to replace the smokejumpers who had to get back to Missoula and gear up for a morning jump into a remote fire. We worked during the night to finish lining the Skalkaho Fire. By daybreak, we had it contained. I had hiked around a corner of the ridge to scout the area, when I stumbled into a pocket of snow left over from the winter. We emptied a couple of knapsacks and started hauling snow to the fire, using it to mop up the fire. We found some rations left by the smokejumpers and realized that jumpers ate far better than we did. We were released from the fire in the early afternoon, and headed back to our base.

At the base, we were met by a woman doctor asking us to drop our pants and bend over. With an ouch, we all received a hepatitis shot. It turned out that one of the members of a Southern Idaho fire crew working on the Pony Creek Fire at the same time we were there had hepatitis. Since half of us had been sick on that fire, it was thought that we could have been infected with it. We found out in another few days that we had merely contracted food poisoning from some bad bacon at the McCall smokejumper base.

With butts still sore from the shots, we loaded up the bus early the next morning to go to the Salmon area for another fire. We arrived at the fire camp, situated once again at the Corn Creek campground. After dropping off our war bags, we were loaded into helicopters, and dropped on top of the ridge. From the ridge, we could look down into the canyon and see wisps of smoke scattered around the hillside. We wondered *Is this all there is*? Since I had more helicopter experience than any of the rest of the crew, another crew member and I were detailed to build a helispot near the edge of the fire, closer to where most of the fire activity had been. The only helispot, so far, was on top of the ridge. If another one could be built halfway down the slope, it would speed up moving equipment and firefighters around. *Cool*, I thought, *this will be the easier job*! The rest of the crew headed down the canyon, building fireline along the flank of the fire.

To build the helispot, we had to create a level spot and clear an area to prevent anything coming in contact with the helicopter blades. Turns out our job was not as easy as it had sounded. We hauled a lot of rock, cleared a large area around the spot, and built a fairly flat pad that a helicopter could land on. Early in the afternoon, I noticed a pine tree candle out. (When a tree becomes completely engulfed in flame, all at once, there is a loud whoosh and a heck of a lot of heat very quickly. This single-tree, complete engulfment, is called candling.) I quickly grabbed my camera and took a photo, thinking that this was all the fire we were going to see on this trip.

Within 15 minutes, more trees started to candle, and then the entire hillside blew with a tremendous whoosh. We looked across the canyon and saw the fire rush up the opposite side. We started worrying about the rest of our crew in the midst of this mess, because they were working down in the canyon. Then we started to worry about our own location, as the fire was also running on our side below us. Everyone was told to scramble to a safety zone and wait until the fire died down, and it was safe to go back to work. So, we scrambled up the hill into the burn and waited. Fortunately, no one was trapped or hurt. In just three hours, this Goat Creek Fire had grown from 250 acres to 1,600 acres. We spent the next three days constructing line and mopping up. That was the last time I ever looked at acres of smokes and wondered *Is that all there is?*

Four days later, we were called to a fire near Magruder, Idaho. Magruder, a campground in the Magruder Corridor, is named for Lloyd Magruder, who was murdered for his gold in 1863. This corridor is part of a trail used by the Nez Perce Indians in the 1800's, then later built up by the CCC (Civilian Conservation Corps) crews in the 1930's. The corridor is part of a 101-mile unimproved road forming the edge of two large wilderness areas: the Frank Church River of No Return, and the Selway-Bitterroot, which is the third-largest wilderness in the contiguous United States. It's north of the Frank Church – River of No Return Wilderness, separated by the 600-foot-wide Magruder Corridor, on the Nez Perce National Historic Trail.

We bussed to the campground, then hiked in to the fire, which was called Cache Creek. We were able to put the two-acre fire out by late afternoon and then headed back to Sula.

We spent the next three days doing prep work for fall burning of some logged units. We working on cleaning logs out of creeks, and building firelines. We hated working in the creeks, because our boots and socks got soaking wet. Sure, we got some good fireline training. And this time of year the huckleberries were starting to come on. But working in wet socks and cold feet wasn't fun.

On the morning of August 23, we were dispatched to a fire in Southern California. While hot-rodding the bus to Missoula, the crew superintendent asked me to talk to the crew about what to expect on brush fires in California. I provided some insight as best I could, but it was plain to see that my warnings and suggestions were not believable to the crew.

We flew into the Goleta airport, then boarded a bus for the city of Ojai. It was getting dark as we approached Ojai, and we could see the eerie red and orange glow of the fire on the other side of the ridge. Shortly, all along the ridge, we could see flames leaping up, looking like something from an old Western movie where thousands of Indians on horseback line up along the top of the ridge overlooking the circled wagon train. Realizing these flames were well over 100 feet tall, the crew began to see what I had warned them about, and that this was going to be like nothing they had ever encountered.

In Ojai, we found a fire camp being set up in a large park. While our superintendent went to find someone who could assign us the worst section of the fire, we wolfed down a quickly prepared steak dinner which served as both our missed lunch and our dinner. It was near 10 p.m. when we headed out to the assigned drop-off point. While we tooled up, the line boss gave our superintendent the task for the night's work. We were to build a fireline to join two dozer lines through a steep area that the dozers couldn't get into. We worked on the line all night, finishing just before dawn.

The superintendent had not been given a radio, so, we had no outside communications. He had us walk the dozer line, checking for problems, while waiting to see if any line officer would come by to check on us. We encountered a steep section of dozer line zigzagging down to a flat spot. It was decided this zigzag line would not hold when the fire hit the line, so we worked on straightening it. By mid-afternoon, we had run out of chainsaw gas and oil, had had no breakfast or lunch, and were out of drinking water. We had not seen a soul all day, and we had completed the task assigned, plus more. We were beat.

It was between 5:30 and 6 p.m., when finally, the superintendent led the crew out. We followed the fireline until it met up with a dirt road. After a long hike along the dirt road, we came to a paved road and stumbled into a Foster's Freeze drive-in, a sure sign we were close to Ojai. We each bought a large soda and chugged it down as dusk came upon us. From there, one of the crew members thumbed a ride into the fire camp. He tried to get a truck to go pick us up, but was told that there was no record of the Bitterroot IR crew on the fire. After basically being told to get lost, the crew member talked one of the National Guard truck drivers into going with him to pick up the crew.

Once back in camp, after a heated discussion and various hard words, the superintendent was able to convince the folks at the incident command post that we were indeed the Bitterroot IR, and had been on the fire since 10 p.m. the night before. Apparently, the people in the fire camp and the line boss our superintendent had talked with the night before promptly forgot about us. Once that was straightened out, we were able to get some supper, and some sleep. Early in the morning, after breakfast, we loaded up into trucks and headed out to the far side of the fire to construct line in a remote area.

We built line in thick, 12- to 16-foot-tall brush, and by dusk, the three IR crews working this area had set up a spike camp. Dinner was flown in by helicopter. In spike camp, there is no camp crew to serve the food and clean up after, so our superintendent volunteered us to be the camp crew. The Bitterroot IR crew was not to be outdone!

We were provided paper sleeping bags, which the rest of the crew had never seen before; I had used these while on the Los Prietos Hotshot Crew. The spike camp was set on TopaTopa Bluff, just a few air miles from the Sespe Condor Sanctuary, where just two years before I had been caught in the blow-up on the Poplar Fire.

During the night, we could hear the roar of fire below us. Since we were camped in the burn, with only dirt and ash around us, we weren't worried about being overrun by the fire. Our built-in clocks awakened us just before daylight, so we put together a breakfast, after throwing cold water on our faces. We didn't have the amenities of a fire camp, but at least we had food and water. After breakfast, and fixing sack lunches, we went back to our line construction. We found the fire had burned up a chunk of fireline that we had constructed the previous day. So, we built new fireline, and spent another night in the spike camp.

The next day, we were told to clean up the spike camp and burn the sleeping bags and any trash, because we were going to be moved elsewhere later that day. We continued to build line, completing our section and tying in with the other crews.

The plan was to fly out that evening by helicopter to the main fire camp. However, that afternoon, we received the bad news that a helicopter had crashed while carrying a crew to the ridge across the canyon from us. The pilot and six firefighters had been killed. Because of this crash, all helicopter operations were shut down. So, the three crews on TopaTopa Bluff had to spend the night at the spike camp without food, water, or sleeping bags. The next morning, the helicopters were still grounded, so we were told to hike out and find the trucks that would meet us. Because the Bitterroot IR Crew was not to be outdone, we led all three crews in the long hard walk out. Upon arrival at the waiting trucks, we were teased because the two crews we thought were behind us had found a shortcut and beat us there.

Once we arrived at the main fire camp, we cleaned up and grabbed some food and liquids.

We learned that our rivals, the Lolo IR Crew, who were being held in reserve at the fire camp, had been given the awful assignment of removing the bodies from the helicopter crash site. We did not envy them their task, and out of respect, our rivalry ended for the remainder of the fire season.

We were kept in fire camp for two days to rest up and replenish our water and food intake; we were able to walk into Ojai and do laundry during this time. I called my family in Santa Barbara, and learned that one of my brothers had been on this same fire, just across the canyon from our spike camp. He had just gotten off the helicopter that later crashed. He was so shaken up that he was released from the fire to go home. We were released from the Bear Fire, which had burned 17,300 acres. We boarded a plane for home.

After arriving at Missoula and loading our gear into our bus, we headed south to the Sula base. We never quite made it to the base. On our way we were called to a fire outside of Missoula. As we approached Missoula from the south we could see the smoke column, and it looked pretty close to my good friends' home up Miller Creek. We arrived at the fire amidst more chaos and confusion than we had seen before. The wind was blowing the fire hard. The incident commander knew the fire was being pushed toward the more heavily developed Pattee Canyon area outside of Missoula, but no one had an idea yet where the fire's head actually was. We were told to start building a flanking line from the logging road we were parked on, and work toward the head of the fire – wherever it was. We started building a fast line, with a couple of crew members burning out behind us to better secure the fireline.

As we worked into the night, the wind died down and gave us a chance to catch up with the head of the fire. About midnight, we had a local reporter show up to get some good fire photographs. But, by that time there was no raging fire to photograph. The news photographer was fairly upset, not having the big fire picture he was expecting. So, our superintendent had us work over an area of unburned fuel inside the fire perimeter, away from the line. We stacked enough trees and dead stuff to get a good fire going, so the reporter could get some photos.

We slept for a couple of hours on the fireline. In the early morning, we continued building more line, hooking around the fire's head while it was sleeping. During the day, we kept on building fireline, even though our production rate was way down – we were just about worn out. That night, a fire camp had been set up, so we were trucked to the camp for the night. The next morning, we were building fireline on another section of the fire, when we learned that a rock fight between two warring Native American crews resulted in the fire crossing over a section of the fireline. We spent two more days mopping up the fire, then were released from the Plant Creek Fire, which had burned 730 acres.

Ten days later I left for college, saying goodbye to the crew and camp.

The Salmon River, Part One

My radio suddenly erupted with a static-laced call from one of the sheriff's deputies. He told the dispatcher that the fire was now into the subdivision, one house was on fire, and that she should dispatch the Salmon River Rural Fire Department right away. Damn, damn, damn. I hate house fires – because someone always loses. Fortunately, I was just finishing up the second critical computer. So, I locked the office up, jumped in the car, called Cindy on the phone, then radioed the dispatcher that I was en route. It would take me 25 minutes to get to the fire area. While driving, my mind wandered back to when I first entered this Salmon River canyon, over 35 years ago.

In May of 1974, I joined hundreds of my fellow students in joyfully closing the book on school, and receiving the long-sought diploma stating that I had received the Bachelor of Science in Forestry. While in college, I concentrated on every fire science class I could take and worked with my advisor in creating a number of credited self-study courses. During these courses, I worked on a few projects with the Missoula Fire Sciences Laboratory. Some research I worked on involving lightning activity was published. Other projects, including an in-depth study of the Romero Canyon Fire near Santa Barbara, and my thesis on the use of remotely piloted aircraft in fire detection and monitoring were graded and filed along with thousands of other student project papers.

A month later, I received a phone call from a U.S. Forest Service district office in central Idaho, offering me a job. So, I loaded the car and headed west into Idaho.

I was hired as a stand exam technician for the Slate Creek

and Salmon River Ranger Districts, of the Nez Perce National Forest in west-central Idaho. The drive from Missoula to Grangeville was scenic, following Lolo Creek up the Montana side of the Great Divide then along the Lochsa River down the Idaho side. Along the way were pocket stands of dense cedar with huge expanses of rock, brush, and snags for miles on both sides of the river. Because I'd studied the 1910 fires – the Big Burn – at college, I knew some of the story behind the 3 million acres burned in Idaho and Montana that year.

There are many well written stories about the Big Burn (or the Big Blowup) and how the hurricane-force winds pushed thousands of small fires into a huge mass of roaring flames, overtaking firefighters and towns, leaving 86 people dead. Actually seeing the scars of this huge fire some 64 years later was something I was not prepared for.

After climbing out of the canyons of the Lochsa and Clearwater rivers, I arrived at Grangeville, the county seat for Idaho County and home to the Nezperce National Forest Supervisor's Office. Idaho County is the largest county in Idaho, stretching from the Oregon border to the Montana border. Grangeville sits on the southeastern corner of a large prairie, called Camas Prairie, up against some tree-covered hills. After leaving Grangeville, I drove toward the top of the hills heading south to my duty station at Slate Creek. At 4,245 feet, I reached the top of the hill, White Bird Summit, and was immediately hit with a breathtaking view of the Salmon River canyon. The hills were brown and steep, with green trees higher up. The view to the southwest was the highlight, with numerous jagged peaks reaching to the sky. My first thought was what had I gotten myself into? Other than a barn perched on a rare flat spot, there were almost no signs of civilization.

I followed the highway, with its thirteen switchbacks leading me down into the canyon, past the location of the first major battle between the Nez Perce Indians and cavalry troops in June of 1877 – a major defeat for the U.S. Army.

After the switchbacks, I eventually came to the small community of White Bird, where I stopped for a cold soda at Hoots Café. It was hot and dry, and the cold drink temporarily slaked my thirst. After another ten miles of driving south on Highway 95, I found Slate Creek Ranger Station.

The combined Salmon River and Slate Creek Ranger Districts, on the Nez Perce National Forest, span an area including the Snake River and the Salmon River.

The terrain of both the Salmon River and Snake River canyons consists of steep slopes, with grass and brush hanging onto rocky slopes from the river up a few thousand feet. Further up the slopes are trees for a few thousand feet, and changing again to alpine high country with scattered lakes and meadows higher up.

The Snake River canyon forms the legal boundary between Idaho and Oregon. The Seven Devils mountains, rising to nearly 10,000 feet, form the eastern boundary of the Snake River canyon. The Snake River canyon, at this point, is called Hells Canyon, and is the deepest gorge in the United States. Geologist Tracy Vallier, in his book *Islands and Rapids: A Geologic Story of Hells Canyon* (2010), suggests these mountains may have been formed from a piece of land mass moving away from the South Pacific, and crashing into the North American continent causing a tremendous upheaval.

The Salmon River, however, cuts through volcanic material, leaving areas of fabulous rock formations. The Salmon River flows from the east to join with the Little Salmon River at the town of Riggins, then moves north gathering waters from numerous creeks along the way. On past the small town of White Bird, the Salmon River joins up with the Snake River. Eventually, at the city of Lewiston, the Snake absorbs the Clearwater River and continues on to the Columbia River and thence to the Pacific Ocean.

You would expect to find very little human habitation in this region of extremes, but, because of the harshness of the area, a certain class of people have been attracted to its remoteness. Over the years, numerous hardy souls have homesteaded here, raising sheep and cattle, logging, and mining. After World War II, the demand for timber for the housing boom caused the Riggins sawmill to be the biggest employer in the area, and it kept the community alive. So, there was long-standing pressure to use the forest and to protect it – for the good of the people living in the area.

Because of the terrain, with its steep slopes and many draws and canyons cutting the hillsides from top to river, a fire in this country can get big fast. If a fire starts in the bottom, it will get to the top quickly. If a fire starts toward the top, it could spread by the rolling of burning debris. So, for the Forest Service, this little stretch of managed lands was considered near the top of the list for fire danger. Fortunately, because the terrain dictated the number of homes, a wildfire in the area would threaten only a few homes, instead of thousands like in Southern California.

As a stand exam technician, I was tasked with driving out to areas that had been logged to check on how reforestation was coming along. As with most Forest Service ranger stations in those days, Slate Creek and Salmon River had several departments, each with specific tasks. The Silviculture section, of which I was a part, was responsible for the maintenance and utilization of trees on the national forest. Other departments included Recreation, Engineering, Range, and Fire.

Because I was single and lived on the compound, I was fair game for any of the departments that needed help on the weekends. I spent many weekends helping with fire prevention patrols along the Salmon River and into the mountains, wherever campers, hunters, and fishermen would like to park or camp. These patrols consisted of two firefighters taking a small engine (at that time referred to as a pumper) and visiting all the campgrounds and places along Forest Service roads where visitors might be camped. There were two reasons for this task: first, to speak with visitors, welcoming them to the area, and encouraging them to be cautious with fire; and secondly, to put out campfires left burning by inconsiderate or uninformed campers.

The summer of 1974 was a quiet one for fires on the Salmon River, after serious flooding during the winter and late spring. The largest fire on the district that year was a fall controlled burn that was hit by some high winds. The plan was to burn some piled slash from a recent logging operation. However, during the night, high winds hit the smoldering piles and sent hot embers into an ongoing logging operation. The fire spread quickly through the scattered debris of the ongoing logging operation. With the help of the logging crew and their equipment, the district personnel were able to stop the fire before any major damage was done.

The summer of 1975 was another fairly quiet fire season. The summer fire crews were able to work the district fires without requiring help from the non-fire employees, like me. During the early fall of 1975, a lightning storm passed through the Nez Perce National Forest and touched off numerous fires. Since many of the summer firefighting crews had left to return to college, I was assigned as part of a three-person crew. We were sent out to a small fire in the Clearwater area, east of Grangeville. We built a line around the fire, checked for spot fires outside the main fire, and then spent the night mopping up. During the night, we could hear a bear rooting around and pushing over small rotten stumps not too far from our fire. Lucky for us, the bear stayed away, apparently happy with the grubs and berries that he was finding.

Mt. Hood

As I sped past White Bird and came alongside the Salmon River, I was finally able to contact, by radio, one of the Salmon River Rural Fire Department engines, Engine 3, and make arrangements to meet the engine at the mouth of John Day Creek. Two of the SRRFD engines had been way up John Day Creek doing structure protection, while crews were burning out around the ranch buildings and main house. With more homes threatened in the Twilegar subdivision, the SRRFD engines were pulled from the John Day Creek efforts and sent to the subdivision. I had about another ten minutes of driving to get to the meeting spot, and I was thinking about the crews burning out around the structures up John Day Creek in an effort to save the structures. Years ago, while working for the U.S. Forest Service in Oregon, I had learned a lot about using and controlling fire.

In the fall of 1975, while still working at Slate Creek, Cindy and I were married. We met at Slate Creek where she also worked at the ranger station, assisting in the main office, and dispatching during times of high fire activity. She had been working on the district during the extremely busy 1973 fire season, helping with dispatch and running errands and supplies for the firefighting efforts. While working in Missoula that summer, I remember huge amounts of smoke coming over Missoula from the west, much of it from the Nez Perce National Forest. Cindy had some fire blood in her veins too! Cindy's grandparents, as a young couple, had manned a lookout in Wyoming for a few summers: one while raising a baby. The story is told that while Cindy's grandmother, with her baby daughter strapped to a backboard, was climbing the rocky trail to the lookout when an eagle swooped down trying to take the baby. Five foot tall, 95 pound, Margaret fought off the numerous attempts by the eagle and finished the climb up to the safety of the lookout. Cindy's grandmother was often alone on the remote lookout while grandpa was out tending to other assigned Forest Service chores.

Because the Slate Creek job was temporary, we left Idaho in February of 1976, for a job in Santa Barbara. I worked fixing up the grounds of a small three par golf course, and Cindy worked in the Los Padres National Forest Supervisor's Office. In the midst of trying to rebuild this small golf course, I received a call offering me a crew boss job at a ranger station in Oregon. So, after just three months, we packed again, and moved to the Mt. Hood National Forest in Oregon.

I was hired to manage a crew of eleven people. Our primary task was brush disposal, which meant we worked in freshly logged areas cleaning up the slash where a tractor was not able to work. Our secondary task was as a fire crew.

The ranger district was called Bear Springs, on the east side of the Cascade Mountain range. Most of the district was of gentle terrain, but the northern edge of the district abutted Mt. Hood, and this area did have some very steep terrain. The western edge of the district ended at the top of the Cascades, and from a place called High Rock, one could see Mt. Hood, Mt. Adams, and Mt. St. Helens to the north, as well as Mt. Jefferson and Mt. Washington, and on a clear day, even the Three Sisters to the south. The east side of the district ended where the pines and firs changed to juniper and farms. The south side of the district butted against the boundary of the Warm Springs Indian Reservation.

Part of the Barlow Road went through the district, bringing some historical significance to the area. The Barlow Road was built around 1856, as part of the Oregon Trail. This rough road carried over one thousand settlers to the fertile Willamette Valley. Less than thirty miles of the hundred-mile road remains visible today. In one area along the highway, if you looked just right you could see the wagon wheel ruts dug into a steep hill.

I recently spoke with a customer having computer issues here in Grangeville, and he told me his grandfather helped the wagons cross on the Barlow Road. The customer also remembered a few other places where the wagon wheel ruts were still visible 80 years later. A portion of the Barlow Road could still be driven, although when I drove it on fire patrols, I was very glad I had a pickup truck instead of a car.

A section of the famous Pacific Crest Trail also passed through the district. This hiking trail runs from the Mexican border north for 2,663 miles to the Canadian border, passing through some of the most scenic terrain in the United States. Two U.S. Highways, 216 and 26, also passed through the district, providing a conduit for travel between Portland and points east. In other words, the district had a lot of travel through it, whether by foot or by vehicle.

At the same time I was hired, two other young men my age were hired to run the two fire engine crews on the district. We three became good friends and were nicknamed the three musketeers. All three of us had experience working on California fires, which was a plus to those hiring summer firefighters in the Pacific Northwest.

We started burning piled slash in May, even before the summer crews came on. On May 18, we were burning some piles along a road one afternoon, when we were called to a small fire along Highway 216 at milepost 79, the first fire of the 1976 fire season. We managed to respond, with both engines between the three of us crew bosses, and a few of the district personnel with fire experience. A couple of weeks later we burned another logging unit with the help of employees from some of the other districts, since the summer crews had not yet started.

By the middle of June, the three of us crew bosses had our summer crew people and had started training. My crew and I were sent off to another district to spend a couple of days helping with slash burns. This was the first time the entire crew was together to work on a fire, even if it was a controlled burn. It was a good chance to see how the individuals would work together and see whether any strengths and weaknesses came out in the open. The Mt. Hood National Forest was trying to catch up on the disposal of logging slash, so my brush crew was kept busy preparing and burning logging slash throughout the summer and fall.

Preparing an area to burn meant the brush crew would go into the logging unit and either build a fireline around the logged area or repair a fireline dozed in by the logging crew before they had left the unit. Many times we would also lay fire hoses down the firelines and place sprinklers off to the unlogged side of the fireline. We would run these sprinklers for a couple of days to add moisture to the area we did not want to burn.

After studying the weather predictions and taking weather readings at the logging unit, we would determine the window of opportunity for the best chance of starting the burn and keeping it under control. Depending on the size of the unit to burn, we might enlist the assistance of crews from other districts.

Once everyone was assigned their tasks, the firing crew awaited instructions from the firing boss, who in turn awaited instructions from the fire boss, now called incident commander. The strategy was interesting, because you studied the fuel loading on the ground, the weather, the firelines, and the steepness of the slope in an effort to place fire into the fuels in a somewhat controlled format. Using drip torches, which held a mix of diesel fuel and gasoline, the first lighter of the firing crew would start a fire five or ten feet from the top edge of the unit.

While that person was at least a third of the way across the unit carrying fire along in a fairly straight line, the second lighter would start out fifteen or twenty feet below the first lighter, and parallel the fire set by the first person. The distance between lighters is a major factor in the fire intensity; wider spacing between lighters will usually mean a more intense fire. If the fire is too weak, all you accomplish is the removal of the small fuels, while the heavier fuels remain. A fire too intense will be hard to control. Once the fire builds up in intensity, the holding crews become very busy making sure the fire stays in the unit.

As the fire starts to cool down and much of the slash is devoured, the crews start to mop up from the firelines and slowly work into the center of the burned area. The mop-up job was especially critical during the summer burns, because we could not afford to leave hot spots that could be fanned by a wind and start a fire outside of the controlled burn.

Burning these logging units was excellent live fire training for the crew. With a few minor differences, the burning operations we participated in were handled just like real fires. The crew had been working together for not quite a month when at midnight on June 29, I was awakened at home by the phone ringing. It was the district dispatcher telling me to gather the crew and get to the station, because there was a request for us to work on a fire up in Washington. I had two hours to get everybody with their gear, equipment, and vehicles on the road. After calling every crew member and kissing Cindy goodbye, I drove to the ranger station. I got as much information as I could from the dispatcher and found that I was to be in charge of a twenty-person fire crew. So my twelve-person crew would be augmented by another eight district personnel with some fire experience. As the crew members started arriving I had them gather water, food, tools, and their gear and start loading the crew trucks. We needed to outfit the eight additional people and get two more vehicles ready. From the little information available, the Gifford Pinchot National Forest had requested a crew to assist with a fire; we mapped out the drive with the help of a couple of the district people who had been there before.

So we headed north, crossed the Columbia River into Washington and drove until we arrived at the ranger station.

While eating breakfast, I was given the fire information and the crew assignment. When we got to the fire, it was quickly evident what was happening here – I discovered we were there to mop up logging units that had been burned the day before. This district had a habit of picking a day, sending personnel out to set fire to as many logging units as they could, then yelling "fire!" and bringing in crews to help with mopping up these so-called fires. Well, we were there to do a job. Even though a few grumbled, we worked and did what was required.

There were a couple of advantages to this assignment, one of which was the opportunity to work in a big cedar environment. Many large cedar trees have a thick outer bark that belies the fact that inside they are rotten and hollow. So, a fire can get into the tree and be very difficult to extinguish. The best way was to carefully fall the tree and then break it up so we could get water to the burning parts.

Falling a rotten, hollow cedar was a job you didn't give to just anybody with a chainsaw. There was a proper way to do it, and we were able to safely get in some practice on this fire.

When we got back to our station two days later it was back to business as usual.

The summer of 1976 turned busy with running controlled burns as often as possible, in addition to brush piling. We also were to assist with manning the State of Oregon fire engine along with serving as a backup crew for our own district engines when the regular crews had their days off. The State provided a medium-size engine, carrying 500 gallons of water and various firefighting tools, to patrol the Juniper Flats country – the area of ranches, grass, and juniper between the Deschutes River and the Forest boundary. However, the State could afford only one person on the engine and for only five days a week. A deal was worked out between the Bear Springs Ranger Station and the State of Oregon to assist with this – not only could one of the district engines respond, but district fire personnel could also be available to operate the State engine. So on the days the State engine operator would be off, the Bear Springs Engine 24 crew would man the State engine and my crew would fill in on Engine 24. I had 150-gallon tanks and pumps on both my crew trucks, so, in a pinch we could respond and use them as engines.

Because our district included two highways, we responded to numerous vehicle accidents. This particular summer was worse than normal, as we had three separate gas tanker incidents that the district had to respond to. The worst involved a gasoline tanker that drove too close to a rock overhang along a climbing grade on U.S. Highway 26, ripping open both fuel trailers. When I arrived with part of my crew, we were in a brief moment of shock at the flow of gasoline heading down the highway. Immediately, the incident commander could see that this was going to take more foam than we had in the entire district inventory, so I was tasked with arranging to meet the helicopter bringing in more foam from Portland. I drove around chasing the helicopter as it was trying to find a suitable landing spot. The pilot finally landed on the highway near the wreck – since the road was blocked anyway. Then, a tow truck pulled into the area and the driver stepped out of his truck, into flowing gasoline, smoking a cigarette! Those of us nearby all yelled at him, and thought for sure we would all go up in a flash. It was like watching the guy in slow motion, but he didn't drop an ash, carefully extinguishing his cigarette in the ash tray. The other gasoline tanker incidents were, fortunately, less dramatic.

A few times we were called to stand by in case of fire and to help with the injured at a vehicle accident. One accident involved a single car loaded with teenagers. We arrived at the same time the Oregon State Police arrived, and we were asked to assist with the injured and make sure the vehicle did not catch fire. The vehicle had gone off the road down a steep embankment, about forty feet. The injuries were not life-threatening, and the state police officer lightened the mood a little by suggesting that the young driver needed to improve his parking skills.

There were a few times during the summer on our days off that I was asked to work overtime and hike the Pacific Crest Trail section on our district. A couple of popular camping spots along this famous trail, especially near Little Crater Lake, had to be checked for unattended campfires. Also, walking the trail with a radio was helpful in case we ran across someone needing medical attention or some other emergency. The people I ran into along the trail were usually friendly, and by day's end, unless I had run into an idiot on the trail, I was ready to tackle the next day refreshed.

For the rest of the summer we were involved in eight controlled burns, ranging from 10 acres to 80 acres. By September 1, most of my crew had left for school, so there were just a few of us left – enough to continue work on piling slash and burning. On September 4, we were called to a small fire that burned only about a tenth of an acre. Someone had been lazy and hadn't extinguished their campfire. This fire, called the Twin Fire, escaped from the campfire ring. Over the following weekend, I was on fire patrol and put out nine still-going campfires.

A week later, we were called to another human-caused fire, called the Sunflower Fire, and we were able to hold it to less than an acre. The next day we successfully burned a unit on our district. As we were leaving our control burn that evening, we were dispatched to another district to help them catch a slopover. Unfortunately, their control burn got away from them. We were given several tasks on arrival. I ended up running the chainsaw all night, while the rest of the impromptu crew dug fireline to keep the fire from getting any larger.

The fall weather stayed dry and warm, so we spent another two weeks working on controlled burning operations around the Forest. On October 2, we were called to a small lightning fire called the Hafta Fire. Then three days later, we were dispatched to another called the Frog Fire. We had barely put this one out, when we burned a unit on the district and spent the next three days mopping up to make sure the unit was out. In the middle of October, we were sent out to another lightning fire, the Linney Fire, and quick action kept it to just a quarter of an acre. For the remaining two weeks in October we were out nearly every day burning slash piles, taking advantage of the continued nice fall weather.

In burning slash piles during October, we ran into the one and only serious problem we ever had in our controlled burns. It was a cool but gorgeous day, bright blue sky, and my supervisor took charge of our burning a large selectively logged area with many large slash piles. We were told to go ahead and start burning the piles, working our way from one edge of the unit to the opposite side. The way the ground was fairly cleaned up and with roads surrounding the unit, we didn't expect to have spot fire problems. We set quite a few piles on fire and were moving along about halfway through the unit, working down a slight hill toward the road and the end of the unit.

I happened to look toward the road and saw a small smoke coming up from a different-looking pile than the slash piles we were lighting. I called the supervisor over, and we thought it weird because no one had been to that area yet to start any piles on fire. As we moved a little closer, we saw that there were numerous stacks of logs along the road, and smoke was coming from one of those stacks.

The supervisor was under the assumption that the logger had removed everything he wanted, but here were stacks and stacks of logs not yet hauled from the area. These logs were pulp logs – not good enough for making lumber but okay for making paper – often left stacked at the end of a logging job.

And we had fire in one of the stacks. Without any means of moving the logs, and having no water with us to fight a fire, we were helpless in trying to stop the growing fire. Soon, smoke started up from another stack of pulp logs. Apparently, embers from the burning slash piles were not cooling enough by the time they landed on the dry pulp logs and were able to start them off. This "controlled" burn ended up costing a lot, and lucky for me, I was not in charge that day.

On November 6, I was dispatched to another district to assist with their slopover fire. I was asked to run a chainsaw and start falling trees and cutting logs. On the second day, I helped with mop-up. That evening I was released to return to Bear Springs.

Once I got back to Bear Springs, I spent the next month burning more slash piles, either as the burning boss, or as a sawyer cutting logs. In one case I had to be the dozer boss, providing guidance to the dozer operator helping with pushing slash into piles for better burning.

Sometimes, the slash piles were a little too wet to start a fire in them, so we would bring a couple of specially developed fans. These fans were powered by a gasoline motor and had a two-bladed propeller of about 32 inches diameter. The pump system injected a stream of diesel and gasoline mix into the wind generated by the fan. We would ignite the flammable mist. With the forced air and constant flammable fuel coming from the fan, it didn't take too long for a fire to get started in the slash pile. As soon as the fire got going on its own, we would move the fans to the next piles. It was slow going, but we were able to burn lots of slash when normally these piles would have had to wait, probably until the next year.

Years later, I found myself working with fans just like these, except they did not have the pumping system. We use these new fans on house fires for pushing flammable gases out of the structure, so firefighters can work inside more safely.

The winter of 1976-77 did not bring a lot of moisture to the area, and the Umpqua National Forest in southern Oregon was trying to catch up on a bunch of backlogged tree-planting jobs during the relatively dry winter. Two of us crew bosses were detailed down to the Umpqua to assist with monitoring and inspecting tree-planting operations, since we both had experience in this. The detail was an eye-opener to say the least!

This particular area of Oregon was close to a well-known (at the time) group of communes near the city of Roseburg. Many of the contract tree-planting crews were made up of members of these communes. Their needs were few, as they survived basically on marijuana and a little food, and the earnings of these members went to the commune. They lived on the job site, usually in some kind of tent, and after a full day of tree planting, they retired to their tents to smoke, sing, and relax. We were invited to their tents, but I would decline politely. We would return to our bunks at the ranger station.

Our job was to watch the tree-planting operation and randomly dig up planted seedlings to check that they were planted properly. The hole had to be deep enough to set the roots straight into the hole, then it was packed so the seedling would stay in position and grow.

I'd planted tree seedlings before, so I knew it was a back-breaking job. In planting these bare-root seedlings, one used a hoedad, a specially designed curved hoe that is just wide enough and long enough to dig a proper hole. After a while, you could develop a rhythm, taking a single swinging dig with the hoedad, and then with a quick pull back on the handle you could open the hole while leaving the hoedad in the ground. With a practiced hand, you quickly remove a seedling from the bag (strapped over your shoulder or tied around your waist), set the seedling in the hole with the roots straight down, pull out the hoedad, and stamp the loose dirt against the seedling with your boot.

The nickname for these contract tree planters became Hoedads, after the tool, and their history dated back to the late '60s.

I remember running a tree planting operation on the Nez Perce National Forest in which one of the Hoedads had a dog with him trained to dig the hole. The dog's owner would point to a spot and say "gopher!" and the dog would dig a hole. The young man would place the seedling in the hole, tamp the hole down, and move to the next spot.

In less than a week, it was too dry to plant any more

seedlings, so we were released to go back to Bear Springs. We both were relieved to head home. The other crew boss with me had the unenviable task of monitoring an all-women Hoedad crew, who tried their best to be as gross as possible. I was fortunate to have a tamer mixed crew of planters. As he and I spoke of some of the things we had seen, we came to the conclusion that some of the stuff was probably done intentionally, to see whether he and I could be grossed out by these free-spirited commune people. Our attitude was that as long as they properly planted the tree seedlings, that was all we should and could expect. For anything else, we just closed our eyes or turned the other way. These Hoedads were generally nice people, but they sure looked at life differently than we did!

The spring of 1977 started out warm and dry. The first fire we had was a State fire on April 5. Since the State fire engine for this area was not yet in service, we responded with our engine and assisted with suppression of this three-acre fire called Pine Grove. Two days later, I was sent to another district to assist with a slopover fire. Then on April 23, I was put in charge of a crew to work on a slash burn on another district. I had barely gotten home and into bed after two days on the slash fire, when I was called to go to another district and assist with another slopover.

Our next fire call was on April 28. A smoke was reported on the district, and we three "musketeers" responded with the Bear Springs engine. The fire was under an acre in size, so we put it out quickly and then investigated. We found a cigarette with a long trail of ash right on the edge of the fire. On the day before, a tree-planting crew had been in the area planting seedlings. One of the crew had apparently dropped a lit cigarette and didn't bother to take care of it. With the very dry conditions, the cigarette started some pine needles and duff to smoldering. The night was dry and by noon the next day, the smoldering fire had created enough smoke to be seen.

An incident during the beginning of this summer led to a

new series of training sessions for a few of us who were trained to operate the engines. The Zigzag Hotshot crew was stationed in a vacant chalet at the base of Mt. Hood, and one early evening the Bear Springs engine was called to a fire at this chalet. The engine foreman was off duty, so the assistant foreman and the on-duty engine crew took off with the engine.

A few miles from the station is a bad downhill S curve, on US Highway 26, that requires slowing down to 25 miles per hour. The assistant engine foreman downshifted to prepare for the bad curve, but was not experienced enough at driving the split-axle shift and was unable to connect with any gear.

Split-axle shift systems are great for giving you a gear in between each gear, so you have more options in getting up to speed. But, the problem comes in downshifting and slowing down. If you downshift a split-axle transmission without using the proper sequence, you not only lose the gear you were in, but you also cannot get the transmission to engage another gear, period. You are then free-wheeling, until you brake to a stop or slow it down enough to be able to engage.

The assistant foreman ended up riding the engine with its 750 gallons of water through the S curve at better than 45 mph in neutral! They arrived safely at the chalet, very shook up, to find that the fire had already been extinguished. Thanks to that near-miss incident, it was decided to bring in an expert trainer from a trucking school in Portland. He provided individual training to those of us responsible for operating the engines.

As the summer wore on, it grew warmer and drier. We had been on two slash burns during the middle of June and early July. The district was getting a few more fires, but the engine crews were able to handle them. On the morning of July 12, I arrived early as usual. There was a lot of activity at the station, with some brown and black-streaked faces milling around. The fire warehouse was open and people were carrying stuff out. Must be a fire somewhere close, I thought, but why didn't I know about it?

As I walked up, I was getting looks from some of the other employees and comments like '*Where in the hell have you been?*' Sure enough, when I checked with the dispatcher, I learned that there was a fire in the White River breaks right on the district. (The White River gets its name from the color of the water, which is a milky color because of the runoff from melting snow and ice on Mt. Hood. The canyon that the White River flows through is the steepest piece of the district.)

Almost everyone on the District was dispatched to the fire during the night, but in the rush, our crew was completely forgotten. I was angry, and I let a few people know. We ended up heading for the fire that morning, and the next three mornings thereafter to mop up the area. The crew was upset, and it took a while to get the crew morale back up.

Thanks to the numerous controlled burns we had worked on, we were in demand across the Mt. Hood Forest to assist other districts with their burning operations. In a controlled burn operation, there were three main tasks: firing, control, and mop-up. As the crew became more experienced, we were given more jobs as the firing crew.

Most units had roads either above or below the unit, so access was easy, but we soon learned to hate the units that had been heli-logged. On these sites there were no roads into the unit, because the logs were lifted out by helicopter and flown to waiting log trucks. So the crews would have to hike in and carry everything they would need. Not only was the access more difficult, but also the fuel situation was more difficult.

As an example, we were sent to the Columbia Gorge district to assist in burning a helicopter-logged unit. We had to hike in carrying everything we thought we would need for the day. Fortunately the terrain was not steep, but the load of debris and brush was very thick. We were assigned as the firing crew, so we had to not only control the fire we were setting, but also work our way through the thick slash and brush. It was more dangerous, because there were no escape routes. If the fire turned on us as we were out in the middle of the unit, there was nowhere to go quickly. It was always good to see a firing plan work like it was intended, and in this unit the firing went smoothly. Soon, we had a large tight column of smoke going straight up into the sky, taking a lot of the embers and heat away from the containment lines.

Toward the end of July, we spent three days working on burning slash for another district. As soon as we finished this project, I was contacted by someone from the Supervisor's Office and asked to do a pre-attack plan for two of the districts, which would take a good month or more to complete. I was apprehensive about spending the month or more away from Cindy, as she was pregnant and due in August. The nearest doctor and hospital were 45 miles to the north in The Dalles, and we didn't have any friends close by that we could rely on to help get her to the hospital. I tried to argue my way out of the job, but I was told that I was the only one left, that the other choices had all turned it down. That sure helped my ego, knowing I was their last choice! So with that in mind, I was able to argue for some considerations and was provided a government vehicle and the ability to go home a couple of nights a week. The government vehicle would get me from Bear Springs station to the detail station and back, but I had to use my personal vehicle to get from Bear Springs to home.

I set up an office in a local motel in Estacada, near the area I was to be working in, and started the summer project. The pre-attack plan I was to develop involved the creation of a map of the two districts with pertinent points of concern should a fire hit areas within these two districts. To develop these points of concern, I had to drive all the driveable roads: tracking the mileage, locating where hand lines could be built, finding places to get water, identifying where a dozer could operate, locating sites for a fire camp, and identifying high-risk places such as bridges that wouldn't handle the weight of an engine. This plan was to be a resource for the teams coming into the area to take charge of a large fire. I would spend the daylight hours driving the roads and making notes, then back in the motel room I would develop the maps.

The project provided a few comic instances; the best was my positioning of a main fire camp on a gentle sloping area with fairly good road access. Looked good on the map and on the ground when I drove by. Although the thick trees along the road hid the actual site, the area seemed ideal. When I mentioned my suggestion for this place as a fire camp, the employees on the district laughed and said they would be wholeheartedly in favor of that. Once the laughter died down, someone told me the site was a large and popular nudist colony.

I had spent a little over a week on the project, when I drove into Bear Springs station one evening to drop off the government vehicle and drive home. I saw my brush crew heading out of the station, and they told me they were to join another crew and fly to Idaho for a fire. I was upset that I wasn't going, but I really didn't want to be gone with Cindy due soon. As I checked in with dispatch, I was told to turn around and head back to Estacada for a fire. My assignment was to be the falling boss on an incident dubbed the Happy Fire. So I called Cindy, then drove back to Estacada, and then on to the fire camp.

Early the next morning, I stood with the firefighters listening to the fire plan and assignments for the day. I was handed ten sets of loggers to manage, more than is usually tasked to a falling boss, but I was the only qualified falling boss available. The task was to walk the fireline and have the ten sawyers and their swampers cut out the trees that were too large or dangerous for the crews to safely cut. As a team, we went from division to division checking in with the bosses to see what they wanted cut out of the way.

After quickly walking the fireline and removing the large trees and logs across the line, we started around again, moving into the burned area and taking out the hazard trees closest to the fireline. With the number of fallers on my team, the job went quickly. We ended up back at fire camp before the rest of the crews.

The next day the assignment was to work with the crews mopping up and falling any trees the crews wanted cut down. I ran into a problem between the crews and the fire team; the team wanted every single tree that even looked singed to be dropped. When looking at the area, there were a lot of big trees that having just a little bit of brown should be dropped, according to the team.

The mop-up crews were concerned with the heavy fuel load being put onto the ground and the potential for a blow-up. We took care of the trees closest to the fireline, but in working with the crews, we left some of the trees in the center of the burned area. I was caught between the team's wanting everything on the ground, the mop-up crews' concern about the fuel load, and the loggers who hated to see a tree chopped up simply to be wasted.

The fire operation was winding down, and the team was starting to release some of the personnel, so I asked to be released if they had a replacement. Under the circumstances, I was released, was able to head home and check on Cindy. Everything was fine, and I went back to working on the pre-attack plan.

A few days later, I heard from the district ranger that I should get back to the station to talk with him about a problem with my crew that was over in Idaho. After they were released from the Cotter Bar Fire in Idaho, and while waiting at the Lewiston airport for the flight back to Oregon, some of the crew followed one of the fire management team members into the airport bar.

Region 6, the Pacific Northwest, had a zero-tolerance policy on alcohol on the job, and the penalty was steep. The policy was traced back a few years to an infamous incident in Washington. The story goes that a train full of firefighters was turned into a bar on rails, with sex, drugs, and booze on tap. Because of the embarrassment, Region 6 decided to come down harder than any other Region, and all team leaders were thoroughly briefed on this. I had spoken with my crew numerous times about the policy, and they knew the punishment was immediate dismissal.

With the pressure on from the District Ranger, I was given the task of determining the punishment for the crew when they arrived home. I had no choice but to fire all those who had been in the bar, as per guidelines. Right alongside me, as I finished firing half of the crew, the district ranger said that they would be the first people re-hired next year. Unfortunately, as I found out later, no one else was reprimanded for this incident.

Two weeks later, when I handed in the work on the pre-attack plan I had finished, the person in charge of the project had a fit when he found out I had not driven the roads properly. I had made the "mistake" of trying to be more efficient. The fact that I had logged all the mileage and kept track of all of the detours to all of the driveable roads was not acceptable. There was one and only one way of driving the roads, and the procedure I followed was deemed unreliable. Therefore the entire project was scrapped! Strike two. My frustration with the agency was growing.

During this time, the engine foreman for Engine 24 on the district took a job elsewhere, and I was appointed engine foreman to fill in – in addition to running what was left of the brush crew. On September 6, we received a call for a fire near the small community of Pine Grove. This was a State of Oregon fire, and the State engine operator was on his day off. The Bear Springs Engine 25 crew took off with the State engine, and a short time later we were told to respond with my crew and Engine 24. I drove the engine, and when we pulled into the fire area, I heard a strange hissing sound. I traced it to one of the tires. Not wanting to leave the engine in the middle of the fire area, I drove it out and parked along the road before the tire went completely flat. I called for assistance in changing the tire, then radioed to the other engine that ours was down, but that we had a full load of water as a resupply. When we got the fire stopped, we checked into what had caused the flat; someone had cut a steel fence post to widen the engines' access into the fire area. The cut fence post was hidden by loose dirt and dust from other vehicles driving over the opening, and I'd driven over it.

The 1977 fire season finally came to an end with some measurable moisture in the fall, so the remaining few members of the brush crew spent the next month and a half burning slash piles scattered around the district. One of the projects involved a special clearing project along the very popular Pacific Crest Trail, near the Timothy Lake recreation area. After the end of the fire season, I acquired a few district people to help with the brush work for a few weeks. A couple of the district people smoked and had to occasionally stop working to have a cigarette break. The other members of the crew were complaining about this, and felt it only fair that they all should stop while the two district people had their cigarettes. I announced that we had three breaks a day: mid-morning, lunch, and mid-afternoon. Smoking was permitted then, and only then. The minute we pulled into the ranger station that evening, I was accosted by my immediate supervisor who had been told by the smoking people of my actions. I was escorted to a room, where I was verbally assaulted and relieved as crew boss. Since he couldn't fire me, my supervisor put me into the building maintenance program. Okay, strike three. It was time to seriously consider whether I wanted to put up with this crap or leave.

As the fall progressed into winter, the tension in the fire section was thick and the district ranger finally realized the problem was not going to fix itself. He called a meeting of the fire personnel to discuss the problems, including my situation. It was brought out during one of these sessions that there was serious animosity between the fire management officer and my immediate supervisor, with me wedged in the middle.

The FMO, realizing I was not the problem, approached me with an offer to try to keep me on at the station. Because I had helped work on plans for a new fire engine, and it was scheduled to arrive soon, I was asked if I wanted to be the engine foreman. I knew I couldn't stay and work after what had happened. The guy causing the trouble was still on the district, and the FMO was already complaining about the new engine and how it needed to be modified to be more like what he would have built.

At the same time, my in-laws had called talking about a business they'd just purchased in Idaho and how they could use some help. The new engine arrived from Albuquerque, and I drooled over it, drove it around, checked it out, wishing I could stay to run it. But the damage had been done, and I promised the in-laws I would help them. So I quit the U.S. Forest Service. We loaded up a U-Haul truck, grabbed our six-month-old son, and moved back to Idaho.

The Salmon River, Part Two

Engine 3 was waiting for me at the turn-off at the mouth of John Day Creek. I threw my gear on board and jumped into the passenger seat, while the engineer radioed that 550 Chief 2 was on board and Engine 3 was headed to the subdivision. The engineer gave me a quick rundown on what had transpired, but he did not know any more than I did about what we were running into. As we approached the turn-off to the subdivision, we could see air attack working hard to protect the homes in the path of the fire.

While approaching one of the homes needing protection, I was thinking that it was hard to believe that the Salmon River Rural Fire Department was now 32 years old. It had grown from two small brush trucks to twelve engines and four water tenders. At least three engines and one tender were working on this fire. I was remembering what it was like when the SRRFD was first started.

We moved back to the Riggins area of Idaho in the early spring of 1978, and eventually purchased a house on a half acre in an area called Pollock. Cindy went back to work for the Forest Service at Slate Creek, while I worked for her parents.

During the summer of 1979, a dry lightning storm hit the area and started numerous fires. We were awakened early one morning to a very weird brown-colored sky, and the air was still with a strange tenseness. We could feel something was not right, like something was going to happen. I saw a sudden horizontal flash out our back window, then an immediate explosive crack that shook the house. I ran outside and could see two fires across the Little Salmon River from us. As I looked around toward the south I could see flames on the hill behind us, less than a half mile away.

Cindy called the ranger station to report the fires while I got our son up and got us both dressed. I figured on grabbing my fire gear and heading to the fire behind us. The dispatcher at the ranger station told Cindy to come to work and bring me with her. So, we took our son to the neighbors and headed to Slate Creek Ranger Station. Cindy was immediately taken into the office to help with dispatching, while I was driven out to a waiting helicopter. I had figured I would be helping with the fire nearest our house, but the helicopter flew me and one other firefighter up the Salmon River instead of toward the Pollock area. We both recognized each other: we had been on a fire together a few years back. We were dropped off in the Allison Creek area above the Salmon River to work a small fire far from any roads. We spent the night on the fire, dredging up old 'war' stories and after making sure it was dead out, we hiked out the next day.

It was also during that year that two homes burned in the area, and there was no fire department to respond to the fires. One of the homes was less than a mile out of Riggins, which had a fire department of one truck, but Riggins' insurance was such that they could not leave town to fight a fire.

One evening in January of 1980, Cindy, her parents, grandparents, and I sat around the table discussing and cussing the situation regarding the lack of fire protection. Cindy's grandmother asked, "Why don't you do something about it instead of just talking about it?" So a few Forest Service friends and I met to discuss the situation and develop a strategy.

Soon we had numerous citizens involved and had started a non-profit corporation called the Salmon River Rural Fire Department. Setting up a tax-based entity for fire protection was out of the question because of the way private land ownership was interspersed with federal and state lands in the area.

We developed a response area, covering the Salmon River

canyon for 60 miles. Using the town of Riggins as the center point, we split the long and narrow area into two zones: a north zone and a south zone. A fire chief was appointed for each zone, with the north zone chief in the small community of Lucile, and the south zone chief in the small unincorporated community of Pinehurst. We held an auction and other fundraisers, instituted a subscription-based membership which raised $8,000 in eight months. We received a matching grant to purchase two used one-ton pickups and two new 300-gallon slip-on firefighting units. These slip on units had a hose reel and fire pump all mounted with the tank onto a steel frame that could just slide into a pickup utility bed.

We took delivery of the two slip-on units in Spokane, Washington, where they were manufactured for us, and brought them back to Pinehurst. The very next day we had our first fire call, and we had to respond with the slip-on unit still temporarily tied by ropes to the engine. Fortunately, the Riggins fire engine had been able to respond out of town for this house fire. They had much of it out by the time we arrived with the rural engine.

With the fire department now somewhat operational, I had to train for a different type of firefighting. My experience with wildland fires was very helpful, but I now had to learn how to fight structure fires. None of our volunteers had experience in structure firefighting – they just had a very strong sense of community spirit. Some of us attended training sessions provided by the bigger fire departments in the state, and we brought back to the rest of the crew what we had learned. In structure firefighting, the end result is the same as in wildland firefighting – get the fire stopped and out. The means by which each task is accomplished is very different, though – one of the major differences is the use of lots of water on a structure fire, and I was used to working on wildfires with little or no water.

Because a structure fire usually involves an enclosed fire – a fire already contained – the tactics of applying water are much different. On a wildfire you can easily get by with nozzle pressures of 30 pounds per square inch (psi) and conserve your limited water supply. On structure fires, you are working with a minimum of 100 psi nozzle pressures, giving you the options of using a fog spray pattern for steam generation or a straight stream pattern for throwing a large amount of water at a narrow target. Wildland engines are usually designed to handle 150 to 250 gallons per minute (gpm) water flow, while structure fire engines have to meet a minimum water flow of 500 gpm. Many of the newer structure engines have rated capacities of 1500 gpm or more.

If you run out of water on a wildfire you switch to throwing dirt and remove the fuels ahead of the fire. On a structure fire, if you run out of water you lose the structure. However, having the volume of water needed to control a structure fire can also lead to severe water damage to the saved structure, if you are not careful. Because we carried only 300 gallons of water, enough to last a few minutes, we had to conserve water. With that in mind, we started thinking about a water supply as soon as we arrived at a fire, trying to line out a source of water close by. We practiced drafting, using the pump to fill the tank from a water source. We started setting up water chances, where we could get the engine close enough to the water to be able to draft. We had the Little Salmon and Salmon River to work with, as long as we could get the engine close. A few concerned citizens set up access to their own pumping systems, which allowed us to refill from their water sources.

Another big difference between wildland and structure firefighting is the protective clothing. In wildland situations, we wore protective clothing designed to protect from burning embers. In structure firefighting, you are working in temperatures that could reach or exceed 1,000 degrees, and you're "up front and personal" with the fire. So, you need protection from both heat and flame. Structure firefighting requires boots and gloves that can protect you from sharp objects, as well as heat. Also, because of the nature of the gases coming off the combusting materials in a structure, firefighters have to carry their own air supply and seal around the nose and mouth so they breathe only the air carried in tanks on their backs. Where you can equip a wildland firefighter for about $1,000, it will cost about $10,000 to equip a structure firefighter. There was no way we could afford those kind of prices, so we begged other area departments for hand-me-down fire gear. With the help of a couple of fire departments, we were able to acquire personal protective equipment for all of the volunteers. Because we worked with the Forest Service on wildland fires (within the fire department response area), the Forest Service kindly supplied us with wildland clothing to protect our volunteers. So, I spent time learning about ladders, large-diameter hose, structural integrity, attacking a fire from inside a building, and the use of the Self-Contained Breathing Apparatus (SCBA).

We learned to work wearing the heavy turnout coat, pants, and rubber boots. The helmet was heavier than the hard hat used in wildland firefighting, and the gloves were heavier and more cumbersome as well. Getting used to these changes in clothing was fairly easy, but the hardest thing to get used to was the air mask. It's called SCBA, for self-contained breathing apparatus, and is patterned after the SCUBA system used for underwater diving.

Because the structural firefighter has to go into a burning building, the body must be protected from intense heat and debris, and even our own breathing system must be protected from both the heat and dangerous chemicals in the smoke. The final piece of clothing is a fireproof hood worn over the head, with a cutout for the face when the air mask is needed. When properly dressed and in an air mask, there is no bare skin exposed, and your air supply is on your back.

Training also included responding to hazardous material incidents. U.S. Highway 95 ran through the department's jurisdiction for 60 miles. We learned about the dangers of various chemicals and how to safely approach a gasoline or propane fire. I attended a few training sessions where we attacked a live fire, giving us the heat, noise, and intensity of the real thing.

One year I attended a two-day session in Lewiston where the instructors set fire to a large oil-covered pond at the airport. We were broken up into teams with a leader, and were marched right into the pond with the hose streams forcing the fire backward as we moved forward. Another great training session was held at night on the baseball field in New Meadows, where we learned about propane fires. A special metal pipe "tree" was fed from a propane tank and lit on fire. Our job was to approach it using two fire hose streams for protection, then reach down and turn off the feed valve and back out the same way.

We also learned about the Department of Transportation's Emergency Response Guidebook, which provides instruction on dealing with a transportation emergency based on which product is involved in the incident. Using this guide will tell you how far you need to evacuate, what kind of health hazards are involved, and whether you can use water on the product. After watching videos of citizens and first responders dying or becoming critically ill because of a hazardous material spill, we all hoped that we would never have to deal with such a situation.

Being a volunteer for the department was tough. The area was populated by many retirees. Those still working were not available during the weekdays, and most didn't want to tie up their nights and weekends. We were expected to be ready to respond to a fire call 24 hours a day, 365 days a year. We had to drop whatever we were doing and either get to the fire engine or get to the fire. While on the fire, we were expected to carry out many of the same functions as the paid professional firefighters. However, we received no pay, and the training we did was on our own time in the evenings or on weekends. So the family suffered, and the job that paid the bills suffered.

During this time, I remember serious arguments flying around regarding the professional firefighter versus the volunteers. Some made it clear they thought the volunteer was no professional, while others were kinder and agreed the volunteer was a professional, just not a paid one. Sure, we volunteers fought less than 30 fires a year, whereas the paid firefighters like those in parts of New York City could easily respond to that many fires in a shift. Our volunteers were like many others around the country – driven by a sense of community rather than by a job. As Michael Perry writes in his book *Population:485* (Harper Perennial 2002), "We study, we prepare, but the fact remains: We are amateurs playing a game in which the professionals regularly get their tails whipped. I fear what I fight."

In 1981, we were able to prove the worthiness of our equipment. It was a hot summer afternoon, when a hay barn caught fire in the Pollock area. We responded with one engine. We knew 300 gallons was not going to touch this fire, but the owner had a working water trough fed by a spring. We quickly set up a plan with the engine operator (our fire chief), in which he would draft from the trough, filling the tank on the engine, and pumping two fire hoses. When the trough was low on water, he would switch to feeding the fire hoses from the tank while the trough was refilling itself. We ran like this for hours into the night, keeping the fire from spreading beyond the barn. The owners came out in the middle of the night with food and drinks for us, a very welcomed refreshment as we had been working on this fire since about 3 p.m. without a break. We stayed all night and into the next day to make sure this fire couldn't go anywhere. After that, we decided on a slogan that pretty much sized up the Salmon River Rural Fire Department – Neighbors Helping Neighbors.

After the experience at the barn fire, we were slightly more ready for our next big fire. Early one morning just before daybreak, I answered the phone to hear the south zone fire chief's wife telling me the Pinehurst Store was on fire. I rushed the five miles to Pinehurst and helped get the engine backed up to the Little Salmon River behind the burning store and place a suction line in the river. We were able to pump as much water from the river as the engine could handle to supply the attack hoses, but the volume of fire in the old wooden store was just too much. We did, though, keep it from spreading to the adjacent gasoline pumps, storage shed, nearby cabins, and house.

After the fire was mopped up and we had a chance to calm down, we were able to joke about the fast response time. You see, the Pinehurst Store was owned by the fire chief and his wife, and they lived next door. The fire engine was parked in their garage.

Later that morning while we were putting hoses and tools away, we found out that this fire had been deliberately set by bank robbers. Apparently, the fire was an elaborate plan to draw the few law enforcement officers from the Riggins area to the Pinehurst Store fire, fifteen miles south of Riggins. The bank robbers then would have no problem robbing the one bank in Riggins. It almost worked, but they messed up on two things. First, they didn't count on a fire engine being next door, so the fire was kept from spreading beyond the store itself. Secondly, and even more importantly, they didn't plan their escape very well. The only paved road through Riggins is U.S. Highway 95, which is north-south, and they had effectively blocked their escape to the south because of the fire. To go north would have sent them right into the responding sheriff's deputies coming from Grangeville. So, they went east along a dead-end gravel road, turned off onto another gravel road heading into the timber, and ran right into a logging crew. The crew had heard about the robbery over their CB radios and were able to hold the robbers until law enforcement arrived. These loggers were a tough lot to begin with and when those idiots stole their payroll, it was lucky for the robbers that they were only held and not permanently removed from the gene pool.

The next big test for our small department was the 1982 fire at the sawmill in Riggins. One afternoon, I received a call from one of the high school girls who worked part time for the in-laws' business. She said the sawmill in Riggins had just exploded. Our department did not yet have radio communication, and we had to reach volunteer firefighters by phone. I called the fire chief, told him of the explosion, and he soon had the fire engine headed to Riggins. Our second engine was also responding from the north. When we arrived, the scene was in turmoil. Two mill workers had been severely burned, and fire was in three or four of the buildings.

The Riggins fire engine was set up near the burning sawdust hopper. We set up drafting water from the log pond and attempted to put out the office building fire. Our other Salmon River Rural engine set up near another building, trying to keep the fire from spreading. We couldn't extinguish the buildings on fire – there was too much fuel for the volume of water we could throw at it. The Forest Service arrived during the evening to help. They set up a portable pump in the Salmon River and laid out hose; their crew spent the night helping us. We were able to knock down the fire in what was left of the burning buildings and scattered log decks.

This fire had both a good side and a bad side to it. It destroyed the mill operation, and the sawmill was not rebuilt. The loss of the mill nearly killed the town's economy. But even worse, one of the two severely injured workers died. The surviving worker underwent numerous painful surgeries and treatments. The good from this fire was the assistance from the U.S. Forest Service that triggered the start of a mutual aid agreement between the Forest Service and Salmon River Rural Fire Department, unlike any in the United States at that time. This new agreement laid the foundation for a good working relationship with the Forest Service assisting us on structure fires and we assisting them on wildland fires.

At about this same ,time, a Los Angeles County Fire Department retiree moved to the area. With his experience and enthusiasm we had a great new training officer. The volunteers received much better training. Some nearby volunteer departments and even the State of Idaho borrowed him for training projects. He stressed both education and safety, and was a good example of what can happen when taking fire too lightly. He was working with L.A. County Fire on an "easy" fire – an overturned car on fire just off the roadway. He and his engine crew members found out too late that the car was on top of a container of chemicals used in the adjacent orchard. The engine crew was working without SCBA equipment, and he had to take an early retirement disability because of the lung damage he suffered on the incident.

A year or two later, on the day after Thanksgiving, I got a phone call at 3:30 a.m. about a house fire just three miles down the road from our house. The wind was blowing briskly out of the south, and the temperature was below freezing. I was the first firefighter to arrive, and I saw the house was heavily involved in fire. A neighbor was on the roof with a garden hose, and I got him to come down. The homeowners had a swimming pool, so we parked the engine close to it and started pumping two fire hoses. We ran one hose between the garage and the house, working toward the exposed propane tank. The second hose we ran along the opposite side trying to knock down some fire.

The fire had started in the chimney on the south side, and the wind was out of the south pushing the fire into the house. The owners had stacked firewood against the south and east sides of the house, and the fire had gotten into the firewood, creating a volume of fire that we couldn't put enough water on. We didn't have a chance.

The Riggins engine showed up and set up to pump from the pool, but their engine promptly froze up in the cold. The Salmon River engine continued pumping for hours – our pump operator had learned on our first barn fire to switch between pool water and tank water. During the winter, the two Salmon River Rural engines were plugged into a tank warmer, keeping the water at a good 50-55 degrees. When the engine operator heard the pump laboring, he'd switch over to tank water to clear the lines of slush, and then switch back to pool water. We managed to save one corner of the house and the garage.

A day later we were called back there to pump water from the river into the swimming pool. The pressure of the water in the swimming pool kept its sides intact. When we pumped the water out for fighting the fire, the pool and ground started slowly collapsing.

A few weeks later, I spoke with the owners, and they were not very happy with our job. Their insurance company, seeing the saved corner of the house, reduced the insurance payment by an amount they figured was the value of that corner! The owners would have been better off if we had not been there, or at least just let the place burn down completely. Hell of a feeling, when you did the best you could, and it actually made things worse.

One hot July day, a sheriff's deputy called, wondering why I wasn't on the house fire he was working on. He said he and the Riggins fire engine had been on this fire for a good twenty minutes, and he'd expected us there by now to help. I told him no one had called, but I would makes some calls and we'd be there as soon as possible. After making a few calls to fellow volunteers, I headed for the fire. When I got there, the two-story house had already collapsed into one story.

The Riggins fire department had tried an interior attack when they'd first arrived, but they were beaten back by the fire's intensity. They were working to keep the fire from spreading up the hillside. We had a running creek nearby, but the best spot to draft water from the creek was threatened by a wobbly power pole weakened by the fire. We needed the power company to cut the power, so we could use the drafting spot. The power was finally cut, and I had the Salmon River engine set up a draft from the creek to put water on the structures and keep the fire from escaping from what was left of the burning house.

The Forest Service showed up to help pump from the creek, so by the time the house was down to the ground, we had plenty of water. But, it was far too late to do any good for the house. About dusk when we were rolling up fire hose, a man ran past me heading for the pile of ashes. I yelled at him and yelled for help to get him away from there. He was yelling about needing to find his dad, and I thought *Oh shit, no one said anything about a person inside*. I found out that his father had died some time ago, and the ashes were in an urn in the house. How was anyone going to find an urn of ashes in a huge pile of ashes? The guy had an idea where to look, but it was too hot to sift through the ashes. I never did find out whether he found the urn intact.

We held an after-action meeting with an insurance agent for the homeowners a few weeks later. The agent hit us with an interesting statement when we told him we focused on the wildland fire potential when we realized we couldn't save the house. He said, "If you'd concentrated on the fire, you wouldn't need to concentrate on the surrounding area." That made me remember wildland firefighting days with the Forest Service – one of the 10 Standard Orders is to fight fire aggressively but provide for safety. Once you go into defensive mode, you can't go back to an offensive strategy.

I got a call from dispatch a few days before Christmas about a truck wreck in the Little Salmon River – with hazardous materials involved. I headed for the Pinehurst Fire Station but was blocked by a deputy stopping traffic. He wouldn't let me drive the quarter mile to the fire station, and I was furious. Just as I was about to leave my car and hike around the roadblock, another deputy arrived and straightened the situation out. He followed me to the fire station, and we put together a plan. We'd been told that an evacuation of area homes was warranted, so I grabbed an SCBA air mask just in case. The deputy and I took off in his car. We went door-to-door warning people to either stay in the house with everything closed up, or to get out and head north toward Riggins, away from the hazmat spill. Then we drove along the Little Salmon River from below the wreck to Riggins, and told everyone to not use their water that night.

Photograph 1: The Bear Fire, 1972. Our spike camp on Topa Topa Bluff. Paper sleeping bag shown in photograph just above my fanny pack and hard hat.

Photograph 2: A single tree candling just before the canyon blew up on the Goat Creek Fire, 1972.

Photograph 3: A Flying Boxcar after dropping a load of retardant during the Bear Fire, 1972. We are standing, building fire line in the thick brush.

Photograph 4: Using fusees to burn out along our trenched fire line during the first day on the Plant Creek Fire, 1972.

Photograph 5: Neptune air tanker dropping retardant between a herd of cows and a fast moving arson fire.

Photograph 6: Extinguishing a kitchen fire in house on South Hall.

Photograph 7: Skycrane dropping water on the Sheep Fire, 2012.

Photograph 8: Air tanker 55 laying retardant strip near homes during the Sheep Fire, 2012.

Photograph 9: Backfiring on the Sheep Fire, 2012.

Photograph 10: Overhauling during a night time barn fire.

Photograph 11: What's left after the Poe Cabin Fire ripped through a forested draw.

Photograph 12: Working on a burning engine compartment after foaming.

Photograph 13: Winter time house fire.

Photograph 14: Structure training fire.

Photograph 15: Two U.S.F.S. engines assist with the Mountain View Road fires, 2012.

Photograph 16: Working multiple fires along Mountain View Road, 2012.

Photograph 17: One of seven structures lost to the Poe Cabin Fire.

Photograph 18: Falling a hollow cedar tree with fire inside.

Photograph 19: Trying to get out of the smoke and heat while attacking an upstairs fire in an older house.

Photograph 20: Heavy fire coming out of a large house.

Photograph 21: Wind blown hay field fire.

Photograph 22: Setting backfire with flare gun on Sheep Fire, 2012.

Photograph 23: Attack engine supplying power company lineman with hose to extinguish lightning caused fire.

Photograph 24: Tree candling during Poe Cabin Fire.

We had no communications from the actual wreck site, and we blindly carried out the requested task.

We found out later that the worry was for only those who pumped water directly from the river. A hazmat team from Boise had arrived at the wreck scene, determined there was no danger, and headed back to Boise. Even worse, one of our county commissioners knew of the situation, knew what material was in the river, and knew the material was harmless. But he didn't think it was his place to call dispatch and have them relay information to us. When I later looked up information on Vitavax, a seed treatment fungicide, it made me even more frustrated. It was not as toxic or as dangerous as we'd been led to believe.

One day, the Forest Service called for an engine to help with structure protection on the Gus Fire which was burning east of Riggins up the main Salmon River. The canyon is steep, rugged, dry, and hot during the summer. Lightning had started this fire in the upper portion of Gus Creek, and the initial attack was unsuccessful in keeping the fire from jumping into another canyon. Fires in the Salmon River canyon are tricky – they not only advance uphill, they also spread in all directions because of the rolling pine cones and other burning debris. A home was situated alongside Gus Creek, with the fire burning in the upper portion of the canyon up from the home.

It was dusk when we got the call, and on my way up there with the engine, I came across a roadblock manned by a Forest Service person. We were cut off from getting to the structure we were supposed to protect. The fire had burned clear down a side drainage to the main road and jumped the road in a couple of places. The fire was too intense to allow traffic through. We pulled hose and cooled down a few of the worst spots, then drove on up to the home.

After a walk around the place, we developed a plan. The fire was still some distance away, with the potential to hit the place from three sides – and all four if the fire hooked behind us. A quick dozer line was cut in on the side facing the fire, and we went to work digging fireline to tie the dozer line into the main road and driveway. We also looked over a spot not too far from the house where we could back the engine down to the river and refill the tank. Our 300-gallon tank on the engine was going to get empty real quick if we had a firefight on our hands. We had everything ready by about 3 a.m. – and then it was a waiting game. Toward mid-day we were released to go home since the fire had moved on and was no longer a threat to the house.

With concerns for our children's education, Cindy and I sold our place in Pollock and moved 50 miles north to Grangeville, a community of about 3400 people and the county seat for Idaho County. I was accepted into the Grangeville Fire Department, but because I worked every day in the Riggins area, I was also kept on with the Salmon River Rural Fire Department. Thus started a new chapter in my fire experience, as a member of two volunteer fire departments.

Double Duty Volunteer

Riding in Engine 3 up the narrow, winding dirt road on our way to the threatened homes in the subdivision, the engineer and I talked about what we needed to do to protect the homes. We could see the fire gobbling up grass and brush, working its way toward homes. At least it hadn't reached the three homes we could see. Scanning the area to get a picture of what we were dealing with, I was reminded of similar 'gobbling' fires over the years.

The Salmon River department had passed its ten-year mark, and we had just purchased a "real" engine from the McCall Fire Department. We'd also acquired, on loan, two 1000-gallon water tenders from the Idaho Department of Lands. Retired military trucks, they required lots of maintenance, but could go just about anywhere with their all-wheel drive and slow speed. We also bought hand-held radios for the chiefs and pagers for the volunteers, so we had better communications. The McCall Fire Department signage was still on the doors of the new engine, when we got a call about a barn fire up John Day Creek.

On a hot afternoon in July, the fire moved quickly from the freshly stacked rolls of hay, jumping the road, and burning up the steep canyon side. On the way to the fire, I heard the fire situation over the radio, so I headed instead for the nearest water tender. I passed the turn-off to the fire on the way to the tender, and saw that the fire had burned up to the top of the ridge. It was now backing down to a house.

The Forest Service engine was heading toward the barn fire, so I radioed dispatch to have the Riggins engine go to the house and set up for structure protection. The Salmon

River engines and the Forest Service engine continued up the creek to the barn fire. I arrived with a water tender and joined in the attack. While we worked on the hay and barn fire, and Riggins set up to protect the house, the Forest Service worked the wildland fire. By early evening, it was contained and the house was no longer threatened, so the Riggins engine was released. Our job was just starting, however. Using the structure engine just purchased from McCall and pumping water from the creek, we attempted to put out the burning hay bales. These were not the small bales – they were the huge round bales. We couldn't put them out, but we'd put so much water on them that they couldn't burn well either.

Unfortunately, they were going to smolder for weeks, and when dried out enough, they would re-ignite. If it were winter or a wet spring, we could have just left them smoldering, but this was the middle of summer. So the Forest Service and I worked out a plan in which a three-person engine crew from the Forest Service would work with me overnight opening up the bales and trying to get them to burn. Then during the day, a patrol from the Forest Service and an engine crew from Salmon River Rural would take turns patrolling to make sure the hay fire didn't take off and start sparking new fires. The owner lent us his tractor with a hay fork so we could move bales around. It took us four nights of hard work, breaking open the bales, spreading the unburned hay and then burning it. The owners came over with food and drinks night and day while we worked.

A common practice in this area of Idaho is to pick a warm, dry day in the spring to burn off weeds while the ground is still a little damp. Ninety percent of the time, everything goes fine, but the rest of the time the controlled burns get away.

The first grass fire I responded to with the Grangeville Rural Fire Department taught me a whole different way of firefighting than I was used to. My pager beeped and the dispatcher said there was a grass fire south of Grangeville; she mentioned the name of the person who had called it in. The roads outside Grangeville were un-named at that time, but directions were usually known by one of the volunteers or a deputy sheriff based on the reporting party's name. At the time, the department let firefighters ride on the back of the engine, so I was in the habit of throwing my turnouts in the back of the attack truck and getting dressed on the way to the fire. A couple of firefighters were riding on the back of engine 2 as it followed us out to the fire. We could see the smoke and could also see this fire was moving fast across a large field. We took the attack engine along the east side while engine 2 hit the west side. I was amazed as the attack engine I was in drove right into the black – freshly burned and still smoking grass.

The strategy, I quickly learned, was to attack the fast spreading fire from inside the black; my wildland experience had focused on building fireline and working from outside the fire. In some places, the attack engine could get close enough to the flames that the nozzleman could operate the nozzle while the driver controlled where the water was going. To me this was not work; this was being lazy! So, I jumped out and started attacking the fire with a shovel, expecting to build a fireline around the fire. It didn't take long for me to catch on that riding in the attack engine operating the nozzle was a heck of a lot easier and covered a lot more ground, so I concentrated on knocking down fire in places where the engine was unable to go.

We kept the fire from jumping a couple of roads and the main highway, and kept it away from the houses in the area. This fire was one of the few good escapes – we firefighters woke up to the fact that grass fire season was upon us, no structures were damaged, and the acres accidentally burned would green up as soon as it rained.

The next summer, the Salmon River department was paged to a vehicle fire along the highway near Jackass Flats. When I arrived, the first engine was there laying hose; the vehicle fire had already spread to the adjacent hillside. We tried to get ahead and along one side of the fire, but it was spreading too fast for us. When our second engine arrived I had the captain drive past the burned-out vehicle to the only house under threat and set up there to protect it. The Forest Service had been notified by dispatch, and they were on the way. We had been fighting the fire for maybe fifteen minutes when we were called to another fire threatening a couple of homes at the far northern end of our response area near White Bird. I told one of the engine captains that he was in charge, and I'd take the new fire. I was in my own car and drove to the Slate Creek fire station. No one else was available, so I took off with the engine by myself.

When I got to the new fire, I saw the White Bird engine parked at the first structure, but no one was around. I drove on to the second house, where the fire was burning and getting close. I'd just started to lay out a hose line when a single-engine airtanker flew over and dumped a load of retardant right in front of me. It was a perfect drop, right between the fire and the house. I started to punch in some fireline from the upper house, following the edge of the fire, when a Forest Service crew arrived. I talked with the crew boss and filled him in with what I knew; he said we'd lucked out because the airtanker had been headed to the Crawford Creek Fire (the first one) and the pilot had seen this other smoke. He got permission to drop on this fire, which was a more immediate threat to structures.

The Forest Service crew were barely on the ground when they got a call to a third fire – it wasn't in our response area, so we could concentrate on the two fires we were already working on. When I reached the bottom of the hill, I ran into the White Bird engine crew taking a breather. They had responded initially, being the nearest engine. They arrived at the first home, a doublewide mobile home, just as the fire started to burn the wood skirting. Their quick action had saved it, and the airtanker drop saved the second home.

I returned to the Crawford Creek Fire and helped with mop-up. A Forest Service crew was building fireline up the steep hillside, while a helicopter dropped water on the head of the fire near the top of the slope. Because the home was no longer threatened, I checked with the Forest Service incident commander and was able to release that engine. With more resources coming in, the Forest Service released our other engine, too, and the fire was stopped at about 120 acres.

During the summer of 1994, the Payette National Forest out of McCall was hard hit by lightning, with numerous fires starting up in old lodgepole pine stands. Lodgepole is a fire-dependent species, requiring fire to regenerate the stands. The cones of the lodgepole are serotinous, meaning they're sealed with a resin; it takes temperatures of 113 to 140 degrees to melt the resin and allow the cone to open and release seeds. Like chaparral fires in Southern California, fires in lodgepole pine country can get huge with furious intensity. One such fire on the Payette, the Corral Fire, took off and headed north to the Salmon River, burning thousands of acres. It ripped down Elkhorn Creek and was threatening ranch structures.

The Corral Fire was so large that a second fire camp was set up at Spring Bar campground, along the Salmon River, with the main camp miles away near McCall. (The area is extremely steep with quite a few side canyons and lots of rattlesnakes. The only road was a gravel one-lane with a few pullouts, but it was being managed for fire and local traffic only.)

The Salmon River Rural Fire Department was called in to provide two engines for structure protection, and a task force leader. As task force leader, I grabbed our assignment and positioned the engines accordingly. We were split up the first day on the fire, with one of the engine crews keeping the fire from getting to structures it had barely missed the night before. The other engine was a few miles up the river working on the next threatened structures. The fire was in between the two engines, and I had no transportation between the two. Our radio communications were poor, so I fretted all day over the engine crew I couldn't see or talk to.

The next day we were able to work together, and we

stayed together for the remainder of the job. We provided structure protection for a nice log house and a Boy Scout camp with numerous outbuildings. (Enough engines had been ordered, so the homes farther up French Creek each had an engine assigned should the fire jump the creek and the road.) We set up a portable pump in the creek and ran hoses around the log house, and we were assigned part of a hotshot crew to help with preparation work. Our big concern was a large stand of junipers between the house and the oncoming fire. For protecting the Boy Scout camp buildings, about 1,500 feet from the log house, we kept one engine in the middle of the camp ready to roll to any spot fire, while we and the hotshots cleared debris and burnable materials from the around the buildings. With the creek as our water source, we could keep our engines full; we were in a canyon bottom, at an intersection of two roads. Our concern was that if the fire blew up, our way back to the fire camp would be threatened. Going upriver, the opposite direction, was more of the windy gravel road that led to a dead end. The other road, even narrower and extremely steep, ran up French Creek paralleling the edge of the fire. If the fire took off like it had earlier, our way out would be compromised. We identified a safety zone near the intersection with room for our engines and the crew.

We were about ten miles from the fire camp, so each morning we would drive both engines across an old suspension bridge and along the Salmon River to our working area. Even though loaded log trucks had crossed this bridge thousands of times, it was still a bit of pucker factor taking engines over it. I wondered if the extra two or three tons of water we were carrying would be the end of the bridge, so to be on the safe side, we crossed the bridge one at a time.

In the evening, we returned the same way back to the fire camp. This was the first time I'd been in a fire camp as part of an engine crew; because it was set up in a public campground, we had an assigned camping spot where we could park both engines off the road. This allowed us to sleep near our engines. I chose to sleep on one of them, lying on top of the load of hose – better than sharing a tent with four other guys who stunk as badly as I did!

On the third evening, I was driving one of the engines back to fire camp with one of my crew riding shotgun; we were the last vehicle to leave the fire area. Along a stretch of road with a steep drop off to the river, I saw the division superintendent parked alongside the road. He flagged me down, concerned that a growing fire was below the road, between there and the river. Apparently, the rest of the vehicles that had passed by hadn't seen the spot fire. The three of us put the fire out, then continued on to the fire camp.

I had to return to working for the in-laws, so I'd been training the new fire chief. I got a volunteer to replace me and made sure the chief was okay with the assignment, then rode into town with the division superintendent to catch up on three days of missed work.

A week or two later, we were called to a fire near Denny Creek near Pollock. An old bachelor who lived there would burn a pile of yard trimmings whenever the time was right for him, regardless of the time of year. His property abutted a steep hillside covered with dry grass and brush. Denny Creek, barely a trickle this time of year, formed part of his western property line. The old man lit a pile of yard debris that set the hillside on fire. The fire was coming up the hill when I got there, and starting to hook around the ridge into the brush-covered canyon.

We had one home immediately threatened at the top of the hill, three more homes if the fire got into Denny Creek, and six more if it changed direction. Access was not good, just a one-lane dirt road curving up from the highway. Past the first three homes, the road got even narrower as it paralleled Denny Creek and then came to a wooden bridge over the creek. I knew the bridge could handle small vehicles, so I drove over it and parked in a safe spot at the house on top of the hill. I had one engine just behind me, a water tender on its way, and a few local citizens with shovels.

The wind was kicking up. There was no way we were going to stop this fire by ourselves, so I called Chair Point Lookout. The tower was in a spot where I could talk to the lookout by radio, and she had both radio and phone communications with the Nez Perce and Payette National Forests. After giving her a quick size-up and a request for assistance, I had the engine set up at the house on the hill. We ran a hose to protect it, with a second hose down the hill to where the fire was just hooking into the steep draw formed by Denny Creek.

When the water tender arrived, I had it stage in a driveway turnaround alongside the creek, between the two houses. I didn't trust the old bridge to handle anything heavier than our engine. The tender was not in a good spot, so we worked up a quick plan – if the fire started cooking in the draw, the tender was to move quickly to the second house, parking behind it and running a line to protect the house. If the fire was too fast for that, then we'd abandon the tender and run across the bridge to the open area at the first house.

There were three local residents with shovels working up the south fireline, which was cooling down with the wind pushing the fire to the north and east. Along the Denny Creek side of the fire, we had a couple of locals helping the four volunteer firefighters. After wetting down around the first house and hitting the head of the fire as it hooked around the ridge, the engine had to refill from the water tender. This was our weakest moment, and we worked like crazy chopping brush and throwing dirt at the head of the fire until the engine got back and started pumping water again.

We had been at this fire for less than twenty minutes when I heard a strange radio transmission. Someone identifying himself as a strike team leader was calling me on the radio to say he was at the turnoff to the driveway and where would I like him to go. I looked down from my location to see what this was all about and couldn't believe my eyes. There were five structure engines pulling onto the flat at the driveway entrance. I suggested they stage right there, and the strike team leader drove up to meet with me, so we could plan the best use of this fabulous boost to our efforts. He put two engines near the second and third homes and had the rest of the firefighters join our volunteers in keeping the fire from getting any deeper into the draw. The remaining engines were staged at the flat area.

The FMO from the New Meadows Ranger District then arrived and took over the fire. He kidded around with me, asking how I liked the response. I asked him where in the heck he got the five engines; he told me that because of the rash of fires on the Payette, a strike team of five engines had been ordered to drive up the Salmon to one of the fire camps. They just happened to stop in Riggins for a late lunch, and when the lookout relayed my message, the FMO reassigned the strike team.

One Saturday morning, the day before Easter Sunday, the page tone went off for the Grangeville Fire Department. The dispatcher told us to respond to a house fire just three houses down from me. I got to the fire just as a neighbor broke the window in the front door – and thick black smoke poured out. I yelled at him to get away from the door *now*; I was expecting a flash fire or back draft to blow out. As he moved away, he yelled back to me that he thought the owners were still in the house. The chief arrived, and I told him what the neighbor said. But, without the engines there was no way we could go in. When the engine with my gear on board showed up in the alley, I joined the others in putting on turnouts and SCBAs. I grabbed a hose and followed the first firefighters into the back of the house, crawling on knees to stay low to the ground.

The firefighters in front of me turned right toward the living room and bedrooms; I turned left toward the library room. I knocked that fire down and caught up with the others. By then the heat and smoke had dissipated a little, so we could see better. I stopped at the bathroom to open a window and noticed wadded-up paper on the floor in what looked like a trail. I filed it away for mentioning to the chief, after we had the fire under control. When I caught up with the others, they'd just found two bodies on the floor in one of the bedrooms. We dragged the man to the living room instead of outside because of the folks gathered out on the street. I went back to the bedroom and brought the woman out. A couple of us went back and found more of the weird wadded-up paper trails.

Someone had murdered the couple and then tried to burn down the house. Fortunately, the house was sealed enough that the fire nearly put itself out by suffocation. The couple of fires that had been dormant in there had perked up with the influx of oxygen from the broken window. Lucky for the neighbor, there was no explosive backdraft when he did it. When you sign on as a volunteer firefighter, you never expect this type of situation, particularly on your own block in small-town rural USA.

About the summer of 1995 while working in the Riggins area, I was paged for a structure fire up Elk Lake Road. The address sounded like it was close to the SRRFD fire chief's home. On my way to the Pinehurst fire station, I met up with a couple of the volunteers getting ready to leave with the structure engine. I grabbed the attack engine and headed for the fire with the other engine not far behind me. We had only about four miles to go, and halfway there I could see the black smoke boiling up. I radioed the dispatcher to send the Riggins engine to help. When we arrived, the fire chief's house was burning, with heavy fire coming out the windows. I knew we wouldn't save this one. We got the structure engine positioned by a nearby pond, and when the engineer was pumping a couple of 1½-inch hoses, another volunteer and I put on SCBAs.

We grabbed a hose and dropped to our knees at the front door and crawled inside. The smoke was so thick we couldn't see above us at all and could barely see a foot in front of us, but we could see the fire's glow. Staying close to the left wall of the living room, we made our way toward the kitchen and bedrooms, where the fire was having its way with everything. I cranked open the nozzle and swept the fire ahead of us, but it was soon obvious that our David versus Goliath approach was having no effect. Something was not feeling right, like the hairs on the back of my neck were standing up. I tapped the other guy and motioned for him to back out now, and we crawled out of the house pulling the hose with us. We had been outside a couple of minutes when I heard a big crash.

We got the just-arrived Riggins engine lined out, then the two of us in SCBAs grabbed the hose again and attempted to go back in. We were checking the floor in front of us at the front door, and it was gone! In between the smoke swirls, we could see that a whole section of floor in front of the door had, completely gone. We spotted a huge deer-antler chandelier on the floor near the kitchen where we had been less than ten minutes ago. The floor had collapsed, because the original construction had an open stairway to the basement. This had been boarded over in a remodel, and the fire had burned the wooden supports out from underneath.

We had a devil of a time breaking into the basement through a metal door, but we finally were able to get a hose inside and start knocking down the basement fire. With three hoses attacking upstairs and one in the rough basement, we made headway against the fire, but the house was pretty well gutted and the roof was caved in over the bedrooms. If someone had been home, the fire probably could have been extinguished in the bedroom, where we think it started from a curling iron.

As a firefighter you almost never think of a fire affecting your own family. But, every so often we are reminded that we are not immune to fire.

About a year after the fire burned the chief's home at Elk Lake, we were paged out to a car fire on the north side of Grangeville. Riding in the attack engine, I could see the black smoke from a couple blocks away. As we got within a block, I realized that the car on fire was my son's 1970 Charger. When we pulled up, I jumped out, fearing that one or more of the family would be hurt. Fortunately all were out of the car and okay. My son's girlfriend had been driving, and she had done a great job getting the two young children out of the car safely. She was now upset, as the adrenalin rush wore off. I calmed her down and played with my two grandchildren, while the rest of the firefighters put out the fire. Later, it was time to start shaking and think about how it could have been worse. What if this had happened in some remote place instead of in town? Thank heaven for guardian angels!

A couple of years later, after an August lightning storm passed through the Riggins area, a lightning fire was discovered outside of town across the Salmon River in the Berg Creek area. The Forest Service attacked this fire, but because of the difficult terrain, it kept spreading.

The Berg Fire had been burning for about four days, and I was spending the night in the Riggins area instead of driving fifty miles home. I was woken early by the pager going off for the Salmon River department. The dispatcher said there was a structure fire just south of Riggins. I was only five miles away, and the nearest Salmon River engine was a water tender a mile from where I was staying. I responded with the tender, not sure how good the water supply to the structure was. When I arrived, I found the Forest Service building, housing the Hells Canyon National Recreation office, was on fire. The Riggins engine was there and hooked into a nearby hydrant, so we had plenty of water. One of the Salmon River engines arrived right behind me with structure equipment on board. I put on an SCBA and went with one of the Riggins firefighters into the burning building. This office was a mobile office, like a mobile home, and it had been old when moved to Riggins years ago.

We were able to stop the fire, but it ruined the entire office structure. While I was still in my SCBA and mopping up inside, the office superintendent showed up and asked if I could find his keyboard and bring it to him. Because I do computer repair, I figured he wanted the whole computer, and not just the keyboard. I found a computer in the room he said it was in, unplugged the soot-covered computer tower and carried it outside. Looking at me kind of funny as I handed it to him, he said, "No, I meant the key board, the board with all the car keys hanging on it." So I marched back in and found the key board with all of his vehicle keys.

We still had some fire in the ceiling, so the Riggins fire chief and I started tearing up the roof and getting water into the ceiling. While we were working up there, the sun came up and we could see the fire across the river that the Forest Service had been working on for several days.

Many of our worst fire calls come at night. When people are asleep, a fire can get a bigger head start on gobbling up furnishings or landscape before someone wakes up to the smoke or noise of the fire. One night, Grangeville Rural Fire was called out to a fire at the golf course, a couple of miles out of town. When we arrived, we found the large shed for storing golf carts was heavily involved. We attacked the raging fire, but with the number of carts, the tires, plastics, magnesium parts, and fuel cans inside the building, the fire was beating us. Watching the fire marching through the golf carts even against our attack, I pushed a cart from the last section of the building just as the fire was breaching into that section. A couple of other firefighters jumped in and helped and we saved the four carts in that section, but that was all. The rest were either heavily damaged or damaged enough they were unusable. When the building was rebuilt, new safe guards were added so another fire like this one would do less damage.

I took a leave of absence from the Grangeville department for a few months; being a volunteer and spending so much time away from the family was taking its toll. I kept my pager, though, in case they needed help. One night the pager went off for a fire in a meat processing facility just outside of town. It sounded like the entire department had rolled out, so I went to sit at the station in case there was another fire call. The firefighters needed some equipment that was on one of the engines left at the station, so I drove it to the fire and ended up helping with the attack.

The fire burned into the sawdust-filled walls around the big walk-in cooler, and we could not stop the fire. The walls were about twelve inches thick and stuffed with sawdust for a very effective insulation. We needed to tear open the ceilings and walls and dig out the sawdust, and there wasn't enough time. We could hear the fire crackling in the sawdust-filled ceiling over our heads, so we broke off the attack and went into defensive mode. We grabbed as much meat packing equipment and food from inside the building as we could and carried it outside, away from the burning building. A small office for the government meat inspector was our last section of the building to evacuate, but as soon as we broke in there, we were told to get out – it was a federal offense to break in and remove files. With all our equipment, all we could do was keep the fire from spreading into the adjacent corrals.

The New Century

We pulled up to a house in the subdivision and backed the engine in by the garage. We laid out hose and checked the area. Walking around the property, we looked for problems, but this place was easily defensible. We made sure hoses were attached to the property owner's faucets, so we could use the owner's water system first, saving ours on the engine for an emergency. There was a steep draw on the south side, and a narrow brushy flat to the north. To the east was the subdivision road, and across the road was the fire. Beyond the house, a steep slope ran down to the highway. While watching the draw for spot fires, I spotted six deer moving up the draw; they must have been watering at the river, and crossed the highway. They looked up the draw toward the fire, and you could see the confusion in their movements. Four large helicopters were flying right over our heads, hauling water from the Salmon River below us to the fire above us.

As we were drizzled by the water mist from the helicopter buckets flying over us, I was thinking of a few fires in the past that also had quite the air show going on.

The summer of 2000 in the Northwest had record-breaking fire activity. Our little area seemed immune to the hectic fire level for a while, but eventually we too got hit when a lightning storm touched off a couple of fires on August 10. The following morning I was headed for a computer repair job near Cottonwood, sixteen miles west of Grangeville, when I saw a small column of smoke near White Bird to the south of me. This would be in the Salmon River jurisdiction, so I called the sheriff's dispatch office and asked about fires in the White Bird area. They said there was one, but it was a long ways from any homes. The State and Forest Service were working on it.

That afternoon, I finished with the computer job and was driving back to Grangeville when I saw more smoke in the same area. I was just thinking about stopping by the dispatch office for an update when the page tone came over the radio for Salmon River to provide structure protection for one of ranches. Because the owner was one of my computer customers, I knew exactly where the place was; I radioed dispatch and let them know I was responding directly. As soon as I topped over the White Bird summit, I could see the fire burning the hillside across the canyon from the ranch. The driveway into the ranch is difficult – you drop off the old highway and go down a steep gravel road for a couple hundred yards, make a sharp left and then drive about a mile and a half along a narrow road carved into a very steep hillside. When I got to the ranch house, no one was home.

I checked the exterior of the house, pulled burnable stuff away, set a sprinkler on the wood pile, and found a ladder and some plywood with which to cover the roof vents. The house was unlocked and I went to work inside, pulling flammable items away from the windows and doors. I heard one of the Salmon River engines show up, and I had them set up as a lookout near the entrance to the driveway, a mile and a half away. From here, they could see into the canyon better than I could, and they could also see the ranch house. They had a quick escape route back to the old highway, and this lookout would buy me a little time if the fire jumped the canyon and started up the same side we were on.

The owners drove in shortly after dark, and they were completely shocked. The wife had left the ranch that morning not worried about the tiny lightning-caused fire across the canyon, because she could see firefighters working the fire. She drove to Spokane to pick up her husband from the airport, and they had expected the fire would be out when they got home. Instead they arrived to chaos with the canyon half in flame. They called in friends and loaded all they could into pickups and horse trailers. Close to 2 a.m., after they'd removed most of their things from the house and we had a plan to stay and protect the place, I got a call to move the engine to another location to protect a home. By this time the sheriff had spoken with the county commissioners, worried about how few resources were on the fire and the potential threat to the town of White Bird. The commissioners authorized the dispatch of a fire engine each from Grangeville Rural and Cottonwood Rural to help with structure protection.

The fire had switched direction during the night and was slowly moving down canyon toward the town of White Bird. My supervisor radioed me to meet him at the Free Use Road junction. He had me take over one of the Salmon River engines and set up protection for a couple of ranches nearby. I caught up with the other Grangeville firefighters and had them set up at one of the ranches. I left them a five-gallon container of concentrated foam, in case they needed to lay a blanket of foam on the house. By the time I set up the Salmon River engine at the next ranch, the fire had died down, so we got a couple of hours of rest before daylight.

At dawn, the fire was quiet, so the Grangeville and Cottonwood engines headed back to their stations. Air attack started retardant drops to keep the fire from burning into a couple of major canyons. I wanted to get back to the ranch, expecting the fire to start working up canyon again, but I had to get in touch with the person in charge of this fire. I wanted to prepare for a burnout, setting fire around the house in case the fire jumped the creek and raced up toward the house. I found the incident commander, but, he told me absolutely no way. He was planning to construct fireline from the top of the opposite canyon wall clear down into the canyon, across the creek and up the other side of the canyon to meet up with us at the ranch house. He emphatically stated that we should not burn out, until he gave the go-ahead.

When I got back to the house and explained the plan, the owner did not like it either. He called a friend with a small dozer to come over. While we removed brush and small trees from around the ranch buildings, the dozer started a fireline where we had cleared the brush and trees. I had one of the crew members borrow the owner's four-wheeler and take the driveway back to the main road, checking the fire down in the canyon. We did not have a lookout anymore, because the engine I'd posted the previous night was now protecting another structure. He came back excited and angry and told me there was a crew poised to set a backfire above us. That meant we were going to be in between both fires. I was livid, and radioed my supervisor and asked if he could get that crew to back off. In the meantime, I went over a plan with my crew and the owner in case the fire roared over us. We had a nice green section of lawn designated as our safety zone, but I felt very nervous about the chances of being caught in this fire. Our location was on a small flat knob, two-thirds the way up a steep slope.

The fire was across the narrow canyon, working its way up the canyon, with rolling material starting fire in the bottom of the canyon. To the right of us was a draw feeding into the canyon, and to the left and behind us was a steep hillside climbing over 800 feet to the top of the ridge. We were as prepared as we could be, and we kept a vigil on the fire and walked around the house and outbuildings as we waited.

A few hours later the Salmon River chief told us to move to another location to protect a threatened home. The ranch owner was unhappy, but we had to go. There was a dozer line all around the house and we had cut down and cleared away brush and trees to make the house more defensible.

As we pulled up to the next house, the engine broke down; a battery cable had shorted against the metal side of the engine, burned out the batteries, and put a hole in the battery compartment. One of the crew had his car with him, so went to get tools and a battery while I stayed with the engine. By the time we got it back in service, the fire had moved on upslope to another home.

We were sent to join the rest of the crew at the next threatened home. By this time, it was early evening and the fire was moving uphill into hay fields, timber, and slash piles from an earlier logging operation. Airtankers had been dropping retardant around the ranch house we were protecting, so the barn and the grounds around the structures were painted pink with retardant.

Before we could wet things down, we checked our water supply – it wasn't looking good. Besides the two engines we'd brought, we had an old water tender belonging to the ranch. But we decided to hold the water in the engines and tender for when the fire hit, and we made sure the area around the house and other buildings was as secure as possible. The gravel road, which was the only access, followed the top of the ridge, and was the separating line between the burning hay fields and the ranch house. The fire was below us, but still across the road. We worried that the fire would cross the road below us and make a run uphill at us. With nightfall, the fire slowed down, and by 1 a.m. we were talking about getting a little sleep. Some of the firefighters left for home and a few of us stayed with the equipment at the ranch, in case the fire picked up during the night.

Sure enough, we had barely closed our eyes for a little rest when the fire found a thick stand of brush and flared up down the road from us. I grabbed a shovel and ran down the road and found a couple of White Bird volunteers trying to hold back the advancing flames. I jumped in and helped them, digging and chopping the brush, while one of them sprayed water onto the fire. We held it from advancing, and by 5 a.m. the humidity had risen enough to put the fire down to just individual pockets of fire scattered around. We got in about two hours of rest.

By 8 a.m., I had two of our engine crews heading up the road to burn out along the road in preparation for the fire, while a third engine crew stayed at the ranch house. The fire was burning on mostly private lands. The Forest Service boundary was about a mile up the road from the ranch house. Here was a big problem. The private land had recently been selectively logged and the slash was fairly well piled up and not scattered. The Forest Service land, though, had not been logged for many years, and the trees were thick. If the fire hit those stands, it was going to crown and move fast in all that thick fuel.

We knew where the fire would jump the road – right at the Forest Service boundary. Not wanting to just sit around waiting for the fire to hit us later in the day, we started working from the boundary of the federal land, trimming tree limbs and burning the ground fuels out from the road toward the fire. Unfortunately, the place that needed the most work, along the Forest Service boundary, was too thick for us to do anything safe in the short time we had. So, we concentrated on the private land area. While we were working along the road, one of the line bosses buzzed by on a four-wheeler and told us we were wasting our time. He was the same guy who had told me absolutely no way to the burnout around the ranch house. I ignored his comments and had the crew continue working along the road back toward the house anyway, burning out as best we could. By about noon, we were reinforced with a large water tender from northern Idaho; we were now looking much better on our ability to protect the ranch.

As noon came and went, the weather was getting hotter and drier. I was worried that our burning might get out of control, so we stopped. A short time later, we were reinforced with a twenty-person fire crew from southern Idaho, a couple of small engines from the State and the Forest Service, plus a small dozer from a local rancher. We all congregated in the hay field across the road; we knew this was going to be our problem child.

Early in the afternoon, we could see more smoke coming from the canyon below us, and could hear the fire building momentum. Soon, we could see flames popping up steadily as the fire worked its way up the canyon wall. Where the area had been logged, the fire was steadily advancing on the ground. When it hit a slash pile, it would roar, throw smoke and flame in the air, then settle down into consuming the pile, while the main fire continued on with the ground advance. I kept checking by radio with the structure protection crew, making sure the fire had not hooked around below them. A couple of members of the crew who had just arrived were patrolling the road below us, working toward the house.

Then, the thick stand of trees at the Forest Service boundary went up in a massive fireball and thousands of firebrands flew across the road into 'our' hay field. The speed and fury of the fire caught us off guard, and in seconds, we had hundreds of spot fires scattered in the field. After a collective *Holy shit!* we grabbed vehicles and tools and went on the attack. The fire had found the thick stuff and it crowned, moving fast and hot. Just what we were afraid of and helpless to stop.

We got the engines and dozer quickly working to punch in a new fireline in the hay field, heading north toward the head of the fire. The fire was roaring through some thick timber, but had slowed down after it burned over the top of the ridge. We were going to try to head it off where it had hit flat ground.

As we got to the head of the fire, there was a yell and then a general exodus of the crews and equipment from the trees. I was running in one direction to get to the fire, while everyone else was high-tailing it in the opposite direction toward me. One of my crew members was in her pickup and saw me running, so she yelled for me to jump in. The fire had blown up again, while everyone was trying to attack it. The word was to get out of the timber and back to the field. We were headed back to the field, but the blowing ash, burning embers, and smoke were so bad, the driver couldn't see the road we were on. I was standing in the back of the pickup to guide the driver, when I saw a shadow ahead in the road. A member of the southern Idaho crew, that had recently arrived, was standing in the middle of this maelstrom! I yelled for him to jump in with me. He had goggles, and I didn't, so he took over as spotter for the driver. We made it back to the staging area. We then realized that if we had cut through the field instead of taking the road, we would have had a much easier time. Bu, we would have missed the adrenalin rush!

With the rest of the equipment and crews also safely back at the staging area, we spent the next hour waiting for the fire to die down ahead of us. Patrols checked the area behind us back to the ranch house, making sure no spot fires had jumped the road. Our section of the road was secure, and the fire hadn't jumped the road.

Quite a few people driving Highway 95, a few miles away, were stopping along the highway to view the conflagration. The sheriff's radio frequency, which we were using, was busy with deputies complaining about stopped vehicles blocking the highway. I was getting radio calls from one of the volunteers and one of the deputies wanting me to send an engine to a structure in the next canyon over. The quickest way there was to take the road through the fire, and I wasn't about to put an engine and crew in more danger than we already were. The only other way there was a long drive down the hill and up another steep hill, and by the time the engine arrived, the fire would have laid down anyway. So, I kept the engines together in our current location. The fire never came close to the home in the next canyon. As night fell and the fire intensity dropped, we took a drive along the road ahead of us, where the fire had raged just a couple hours ago.

It was eerie in the dark, with thousands of individual flames licking away at what was left of a once forested hillside. Before afternoon, the fire had burned mostly grass and brush, but it was now firmly entrenched in the timber. It was going to be a long hard battle. Because the fire had burned past the homes, I handed over command of our crews and headed home.

A week later, I was called in to replace a crew member still working on this fire, dubbed the Burnt Flats Fire. We were assigned to help mop up along the main road, freeing up the state and federal engines, so they could work the tougher areas of the fire.

Major fires were burning throughout Idaho and Montana, and resources were stretched extremely thin. A fire management team from Australia was brought in to learn and to assist the Blue Mountain incident management team on this Burnt Flats fire. We didn't get a chance to meet them, because we were not working at the head of the fire, which is where they were concentrating their efforts. After about twenty days the Salmon River department was released from the fire. The fire burned 22,527 acres and cost just under $8 million to control.

On September 8, 2001, the forest outside Grangeville was hit by an arsonist. In the early afternoon, I was working on a computer repair job just west of town when I heard one of the single-engine airtankers (SEATs) fly overhead. I could see smoke coming from what looked like the top of White Bird Hill, about nine miles south. Because I hadn't heard a call-out for the Grangeville department, I figured it must be outside of our jurisdiction.

Later that day, Grangeville Rural Fire Department was toned out to a fire past Mt. Idaho near the refuse transfer station. Since I was now in this area, I responded directly in my car. When I arrived, I noticed a couple of Forest Service people working a small fire just off the road below the summit. There was a larger smoke coming from farther down the grade. I headed there, took a quick look, drove past the fire to turn around and parked in a safe area.

I could hear what sounded like a fire crackling, but it seemed to come from below me. Walking around the car, I spotted a third fire below me in the draw. I didn't want to get caught between the two fires, so I moved my car and made sure it was ready to get out of there in a hurry. There was no cell phone signal here, I had no radio, so I couldn't tell anyone about the situation. A helicopter flew overhead with a water bucket and dropped water on the fire below me. I figured the pilot was able to radio what was going on. I started working along the edge of the second fire, building fireline from the road uphill along the fire's edge. Just then a couple of the SEATs airtankers started working right above me. A Forest Service engine pulled up and took over from me. Then I headed up the hill to find the Grangeville crew. The nearest homes were not immediately threatened, and the concern was for a herd of cows out in an open field. One of the larger airtankers dropped a load of retardant between the fire and the cows, slowing the fire's advance; the cows didn't seem bothered and wandered off away from the fire. The fire was burning away from the scattered homes. As more state and federal equipment arrived, we were released from the fire.

We learned later that the arsonist fires had touched off eleven fires in just a few days. That fire I'd thought was on top of White Bird summit was, indeed, on the very edge of the Salmon River jurisdiction, and had threatened a couple of homes. From the looks of the fires' ignition points, the arsonist knew what he was doing. Months later, after a lot of investigative work, the arsonist was caught.

September 11, 2001- a terrible day for the United States. I am sure none of us will forget the videos of the planes crashing into the Twin Towers and the resulting collapse, or the photographs of the Pentagon crash site and the one in Pennsylvania. Once the news of the tragic loss of lives from the attack was sorted out, fire departments across the country held memorial services for those killed in the incidents.

The Grangeville Fire Department was asked to honor those killed by parading three engines, one carrying the American flag, through town. The Forest Service had a fire camp set up at the edge of town, and it was decided to include these firefighters in the memorial service. It was a sad occasion, as we drove through town like a funeral procession, with a couple of police and sheriff escorts followed by our antique fire engine carrying the flags, then by a Grangeville City fire engine, a Grangeville Rural engine, a contract fire engine from Minnesota working on the wildfire, and a

Nezperce National Forest wildland engine. We drove through the fire camp too, including them in our brief memorial. The whole community came to a standstill and watched as we drove the flag as an honor to those who had perished. Although all airports in the United States had been shut down, Grangeville airport remained open due to the fire fighting traffic.

The Grangeville department trains twice a month in the evening, and when the weather is good we train outdoors. One summer evening found us with all of the engines, both city and rural, driving out to a potentially nasty area called the Fish Hatchery. A lot of homes are scattered in the timber, and the gravel roads are narrow and occasionally steep. We drove the area, taking note of how much room there was for the engines and doing some pre-attack planning and narrow road driving practice.

On our way back to town, we had to stop for a pickup hauling a horse trailer and a semi truck stopped alongside the pickup, completely blocking the road. I was in the first engine, closest to the stopped vehicles, patiently waiting for them to move. Suddenly, the semi started up and drove into the side of the horse trailer, then pulled off to the opposite side of the road and stopped. All of us in the engine, in unison, said *"Holy shit, what the hell was that?"* A couple of the volunteers jumped from the engine, while I radioed dispatch to report an accident and the need for a deputy.

The woman driving the pickup came running, extremely upset and worried about her horse in the trailer. She said her ex-husband was angry – he was the semi driver who had purposely crashed into her horse trailer. The guy was walking toward us. One of the volunteers grabbed a fire axe, while we got the woman inside the cab of the engine. A few more volunteer firefighters walked up from the stopped engines behind us, wondering what the heck was going on. They hadn't seen the incident, and when I had radioed dispatch they thought our engine was involved in the accident.

A couple of the volunteers ran over to the horse trailer to make sure the horse was okay – it was – and the angry ex-husband kept trying to get around us wanting to talk to the woman we had in the engine. We managed to keep him at bay until a deputy arrived. This type of training is never in the cards, but it reminded us that "shit happens". You never know what to expect.

One cold winter morning, Salmon River Rural was paged for a hazmat incident – a vehicle accident on the Time Zone bridge just north of Riggins, with leaking fuel. I drove to the Rapid River Fire Station, threw a few bags of absorbent in the back of Engine 33, and headed for the accident. When I radioed in that I'd arrived, I couldn't believe the mess in front of me. A semi truck was going too fast across the bridge and had lost control on a patch of ice. It crashed into the cement barrier on the edge of the northbound lane, bounced up, plowed into the steel support arch of the bridge, then came down onto the highway, scattering pieces everywhere.

The cab had sheared off and was lying on its side near the guardrail on the northbound lane, while the cab-less chassis was some thirty feet away straddling the highway. The trailer was jackknifed close to the chassis but still upright. One fuel tank was lying in the weeds on the south side of the highway while the other was leaking badly on the highway. I'd heard over the radio that the driver was in the ambulance on the way to the hospital, so I just needed to worry about the fuel.

The Salmon River was below the bridge, and the highway vents would drain the spilled fuel right into the river. I started spreading the absorbent I had with me, working around the drain vents first to stop the flow of diesel heading for the river.

Engine 11 from Pinehurst Station arrived with a few more sacks of absorbent, and they helped me spread it to check the flow in other places. Where there was loose dirt, we used that to build dikes to channel fuel into a depression where we could dump more absorbent later. The fire chief was on the way, so I radioed him to stop and grab more absorbent. A couple of us crawled down onto the boulders below the bridge to make sure no fuel had leaked down from the bridge. The fuel and antifreeze had barely dripped down onto a pocket in the boulders, and we dumped absorbent there to take care of the puddle. We finally had the entire area covered with absorbent. Once the tow trucks arrived, we started sweeping and shoveling the used absorbent back into the sacks for disposal.

A few days later in the local newspaper story on the accident, the state police officer in charge praised the fire department personnel for our work in keeping fuel out of the river. The truck driver was fine; he actually walked away from the cab. The fuel was caught and removed, so all was well. Of course the truck was in pieces, but trucks can be replaced.

During one of the busy wildfire seasons, Grangeville was paged out to an aircraft emergency at the airport. We met up with the Forest Service air base manager, who told us a helicopter was in trouble. It was on its way in from working a fire out of Elk City and that it was experiencing engine problems. The pilot was afraid to release his water bucket, since he would have to lose altitude to do so. He was fighting the controls, and it was going to be worse if he lost altitude. Therefore, he kept the helicopter at a safe height, dragging the water bucket, trying to bring the helicopter to Grangeville, where we were waiting. The chief and the base manager worked out a plan. With a Forest Service radio in hand, the chief told us to ready both of the rural engines – they can pump foam on the run.

Soon, we could see the helicopter coming in from the east. Once the pilot fought the helicopter to the east end of the runway, he was able to jettison the water bucket. As he flew over the runway headed for the first helipad, we paralleled him with the attack engine. I was standing in the back handling the foam nozzle with another guy working the pump. We focused on the pilot, waiting for a sign that we needed to spray foam. As he brought the helicopter onto the ground, both rural engines stood by, nozzles at the ready. The pilot was able to land and shut everything down, and gave us the thumbs-up that all was fine. We shut down our pumps and headed back to the fire station

Months later, I was working in Riggins and had made arrangements with one of the volunteer firefighters there to train me on using the newly acquired Salmon River Engine 3. The fire chief, a retired firefighter from another state, had worked out a deal with the department he had retired from to acquire a surplus engine when one came available. He had picked up the engine a couple of months before, and firefighters had repaired some problems to get the engine in service. This engine was stationed at the Rapid River fire station, just a mile from me at the time.

It was about 5 p.m., when the other firefighter was to meet me with the engine. I saw a sheriff's deputy drive by with flashing lights heading south. I made sure my pager was open and heard something about a fire and the Salmon River fire department. So, I phoned dispatch to ask if there was a fire in the area, and she said there was a fire threatening homes up Elk Lake Road. Jumping into my car, I headed to the fire.

The closest house was being protected by one of our engines, while a second engine was held in reserve for water supply. I got a quick status report from one of the Salmon River captains on the fire. The trouble spot was the head of the fire, moving up the hill. One member of the crew was alone at the top of the fire, so I got a ride on a four-wheeler up there to help him hold the fire from spotting across a narrow dirt road. We started working down the hill from the road, putting out fires. The Forest Service's New Meadows Ranger District engine arrived, and between both of our forces, we were able to stop the fire from growing beyond a few acres.

The next afternoon, I was driving out of Riggins past the turn-off to the Rapid River fire station when my radio pager again picked up something about the Salmon River fire department. When I got to the office, a mile away, I phoned the dispatch office. The dispatcher said there was a fire up Race Creek, about seven miles away. I told her I'd respond with the Rapid River engine. I started up Engine 3 and waited a couple of minutes, then took it by myself when no one else showed up.

While driving with lights and siren on Highway 95 headed to the fire, I kept thinking to myself, "I hope someone else shows up who knows how to run this engine," since my training the night before had been postponed by the fire up Elk Lake Road. I slowed as I pulled into the town of Riggins, and up ahead of me were two Salmon River volunteer firefighters standing in the middle of the street. I barely stopped to let them on. As we continued toward the fire I filled them in with the little I knew about the fire. Both had been working on a private vehicle and hadn't heard the page either, but they could hear my siren coming. When they saw the engine, they knew to get on. Luckily for me, they both knew how to operate the engine!

We headed up Race Creek and met a sheriff's deputy who told us the fire was burning in a blackberry patch. We could either drive across a field to get to it or head up the road a short distance to the first threatened house. Taking a quick look, I said we were going to the house. No sooner had we started toward the house when the fire roared out of the blackberries and headed for that first house.

The driveway was blocked by a locked gate, and no one had a key. The sheriff's deputy tried to break the chain but couldn't. The nearest neighbor saw our predicament and brought over his tractor. While he was working to lift the gate out, I ran up the driveway to see how bad the road was and get a better idea of what we were taking the engine into. It looked as though no one had used this driveway for quite a while, but it was the only way to the house. I didn't want to get the engine stuck or jammed up on the driveway, but we needed it at the house. As soon as the gate was removed, I had the neighbor bring his tractor up the driveway to remove rocks and debris. Riding on the tractor, with Engine 3 following, we arrived at the threatened house. The neighbor headed back home with his tractor while we positioned the engine.

We ran hoses along two sides of the house. Another Salmon River volunteer radioed that he was going through Riggins headed our way. He didn't have an engine with him, so I asked him to go get the nearest Salmon River engine and bring it as soon as possible. I was afraid we were going to have a couple more homes threatened shortly.

By now, a couple of Forest Service firefighters had arrived. One of them came up the hill and tied in with us. He had knocked down some of the worst spots of advancing fire, and gave us a short report on the fire below us. He then took off up the hill to catch up with the fire that had already burned past one side of this house. The finger of fire that had gone past us kept going uphill, and the rest of the advancing fire was a little slower. It was spreading uphill instead of sidehilling, so the next nearest house was safe unless the wind changed. As the fire was working toward the house, we hit the flames with water and wet down the green junipers alongside the house. We didn't want those junipers catching fire, because the heat and embers from them could set the house afire.

Once we got the junipers wet and knocked down the fire closest to the house, the nozzleman headed downhill following the edge of the fire. In the meantime, the second Salmon River engine arrived, but needed one of my crew to help. By this time, the two of us could handle the fire near the house, so I sent the third firefighter down the hill to help with Engine 4. They worked on the fire threatening a house near where the fire had started.

More Forest Service firefighters arrived with a couple of engines and a helicopter. The fire now was headed up the hill into the forest. Once the threat to the homes was removed, and the fire was starting to die down for the evening, we were released. The next day it rained a little, which helped the Forest Service put the fire completely out.

I felt sorry for the older gentlemen who had started the fire, for he was given some bad advice by someone in Riggins. He had asked around in town about whether this was a good time to burn the blackberry patch on his property and someone had told him "yep, no problem." Unfortunately, no one warned him that blackberries burn fast and hot even when they are green. It was an expensive lesson for him.

Later that fall, in the midst of a gorgeous Indian Summer, we had a wind event hit the Poplar Drive area outside of the community of Mt. Idaho. Arcing powerlines ignited a fire. Dispatch paged out Grangeville, and I responded directly in my car. The wind was pushing the fire toward five homes sitting down in a 'bowl', with a few more homes at the top of the 'bowl'. As I pulled up to the house closest to the approaching fire, the owner was running out from the woods where he'd had a quick look at the fire. He said it was coming fast, so I helped them evacuate. We got their house and garage closed up. When the Grangeville attack engine arrived, we contacted the other residents in the 'bowl' and helped them get out.

One of the homes belonged to a member of the Grangeville crew, and we helped set up a defense at his house. We removed flammable items from close to the house, took a weedeater and quickly cut down some tall weeds, and then laid out some fire hose. By then, the Forest Service was arriving. A large airtanker from Oregon came in and dropped a load of retardant to protect the homes. Most of the Grangeville crew had not been close to a retardant drop before, so when the tanker came in low right over our heads, it was quite the experience for them. Of course no one had a camera handy!

The winds died down as it grew dark. We then had a chance to go in with the Forest Service and start putting out fires near the homes. Fortunately, no structures were burned, but the fire did come very close to two of the homes.

It was almost winter in Grangeville, when I was awakened

late at night by the pager announcing a structure fire on the north side of town, in one of the small trailer parks next to an airplane engine repair complex. We were worried that this fire could get big if it burned into the repair facility. After we hooked into the nearest hydrant, we ran hose lines to the burning trailer. The young man renting the trailer, along with a couple of his friends, yelled at us and tried to grab one of the hoses. They were agitated, thinking that we were not getting water on the fire quickly enough. We yelled for a police officer, and even he had a difficult time keeping the guy and his friends out of our way. A couple of us wanted to turn the hoses onto him and claim we had briefly lost control of the nozzle. We kept the fire from spreading to the nearby trailers and the airplane repair facility, but couldn't save the trailer. It was heavily involved when we arrived, and there wasn't much we could do. The renter lost everything. When we got back to the station , we all talked about the guy and how we were angered by the way he'd treated us – but we also felt terrible about his losing everything he owned.

Blackerby

While waiting for the fire to come to the house we were protecting, I watched a hotshot crew building fireline up the hillside above us, and another hotshot crew lighting the hillside on fire along the main dirt road. Watching the firing crew, I noticed they were using a technique I wish I'd had many years before – they were using flare guns, which allowed them to start fires quite a ways out in front.

Salmon River's Engine 2, which had been farther into the subdivision than we were, caught up with us and told us their story. They had arrived before we did and went to the structure that the deputy had called in as being on fire. The structure that was burning, though, was not the house, just an outbuilding. None of the other structures in the subdivision were on fire. That put all of us in a lighter mood, knowing that someone's home did not burn.

The homeowners were kind enough to provide us with drinks and snacks while they waited with us for the firing to pass by. Until it got dark, helicopters kept flying buckets of water over us, keeping the fire inside the firelines and the road.

Both firing operations came together as planned. As the red glowing hillside faded away to just pockets of red, we were released to go home with instructions to come back early in the morning. I headed back to Grangeville for some dinner, shower, and sleep. On the way, I thought about a fire outside of Grangeville a few years before that had required structure protection for numerous homes.

While much of the West had been suffering through bad fire seasons for a few years, the Grangeville area had been seemingly immune from large fires - until 2005. It was August

9, and I was working in Riggins when Cindy called, late in the afternoon, asking whether I had my fire radio on. The radio reception was poor there, and I hadn't heard any traffic. Cindy told me I had better come up to Grangeville - now. She'd seen the two Grangeville engines leave town and had heard airtankers and helicopters flying. I drove back to Grangeville, and when I neared town, I could see where the smoke column was coming from. I knew there were numerous homes in that area; I got to the fire station and radioed the chief to let him know where I was. He and the first assistant chief were already out on the fire, so as second assistant chief I was in charge of the rest of the crew to deal with any other fires that might occur during the night. The chief said he had no radio contact with anyone on the fire, but that we could communicate through our own radio system and with the sheriff's dispatcher.

I then called the Idaho Department of Lands office, since this fire was in their jurisdiction, to see about getting a radio that we could use to talk with them and the Forest Service personnel on the fire. They said no radios were available and they were indignant that we were on the fire without communications. I started to argue that we had communications with the sheriff's dispatch, just not with anyone actually on the fire and that we had been assigned to protect structures. We were not about to abandon them until we were told to or the fire forced us to. After listening to a few more "You should not be there" statements, I finally hung up, knowing this conversation was going nowhere.

Throughout the night I dozed with one ear tuned to the radio traffic. Around 5 a.m., Cindy and another firefighter's wife put together food, coffee, and other drinks, and I drove out to the fire and caught up with the crew. They had had nothing to eat or drink all night, so they were glad to see me. I went back to town and rounded up replacements for the crew. We headed back to the fire, and took over the day shift for the Grangeville structure protection assignment. The fire stayed fairly calm during the morning and gave us a chance to look over the situation at the three houses we were protecting. I spoke with the owner of one of the homes, telling him we needed to move the wood pile and cut down some trees to protect his house. This was not acceptable to the homeowner. However, we did agree to postpone this protective work until the fire moved closer.

Early in the afternoon, the fire was starting to kick up. I hitched a ride with the homeowner on his four-wheeler to scout out the fire below his house. I could see the fire activity was increasing, but the fire was still far enough away to not be worried about it just yet.

A short time later a hotshot crew arrived, and without saying hi or boo to anyone, jumped in with their saws and tools and started cutting trees and throwing firewood. We joined in to help. By the time we finished, we had apparently grown in the opinion of the hotshot crew from hillbilly volunteers to firefighters, because they actually started talking with us.

Once finished with the initial protection work, the hotshots moved on to their next assignment. I took off with one of the other crew members to scout the road to the west heading toward more houses.

The previous night when the fire had blown up from the bottom of the canyon, part of it came roaring up to the road not far from the homes we were protecting. Across the road was a home in the trees, with brush between it and the road. This house would have been a very nasty one to try to save, but two things happened to save it. First, a large airtanker from Oregon dropped a load of retardant right along the road between the fire and the house. Second, right after the retardant drop, the hot sun dropped behind the trees to the west just before dusk settled in. The combination of the retardant and the slight drop in temperature and moisture kept the fire from jumping the road, saving the house, and keeping the fire from getting into even more fuel.

A little farther down the road was another interesting story. The next house was built on the slope just below the road and had black, burned grass and brush around it. But, the owner had kept the brush and weeds down around the house so when the fire burned into the area, it lost some intensity when it hit the lesser fuel concentration. The burn pattern of the fire was obvious as it split around the house, but there were enough cleared areas along the edge of the house that the fire could not touch it. The owner had also been diligent about clearing burnable materials from the porch and roof, so there wasn't a place for embers to get a hold. This house was spared, thanks to efforts of the owner and the work done earlier.

Farther along the road, we could see a few more homes scattered in the trees, with the fire still quite a way down the hill. We turned around and headed back to join the rest of the crew to get ready for the late afternoon fire run.

Soon, there was a huge column of smoke churning to the southwest, but some distance from our location. We found out from one of the Forest Service people that the fire had jumped the South Fork of the Clearwater River and was making a run up the opposite hillside from us. As dusk fell we were notified that the fire was making a major run about a mile up the road from us and threatening homes there.

Since the fire was pushing to the south west, away from our houses, we headed both engines toward the new fire threat. We split up, each engine taking a structure and putting out spot fires. In the middle of this fight, the fire chief brought in the replacements for the night shift, and I made arrangements to be back in the morning with the day crew.

A fire camp had been assembled just outside of town and the next morning I attended the morning briefing. I was remembering my days with the Forest Service, lining out sack lunches, water, and supplies while getting the day's assignment. We were told that this fire, called the Blackerby Fire, was the number one priority fire in the United States currently because of the number of threatened structures. In the middle of the briefing, my pager went off, and the sheriff's dispatcher said a house was threatened by this same fire, but in a totally different area. The fire chief radioed that both engines would start heading that way. I told the incident commander what was happening and that I had to leave the briefing to meet up with my engines. He said he would see about getting some help our way, and I quickly finished collecting food and water. I was also able to grab a fire radio from the radio tech in the fire camp, so we finally had some communications with incident command staff. After getting hold of the day crew and changing the plans for where we'd meet, I headed out to the new location. Once all the day crew were present, we were able to send the night shift home and take over.

Our situation involved a nice house and garage built onto a narrow ridge, with a draw to the right side and a deep canyon on the left. We had three more homes in the vicinity that we needed to protect. We removed brush and saplings from the garage area while walking around the place to see what other problems we'd have to deal with. The fire had hooked around farther down the ridge and had burned part of the ridge before dying down. Part of the fire had crept up from the draw and actually burned right up to the house, which was surrounded by a wood deck. The fire had burned the grass under the deck on the draw side of the house. Luckily the owners had cleared everything but just light grass from under the deck. We made sure the fire was out down there and that no wooden pillars were charred or had hidden fire in them.

One of the other crew members and I took the attack engine for a drive to the other homes that we had to protect. We needed to scout what we needed to do to prepare for the fire. The fire had pretty well established itself in the lower portion of the draw, so we were expecting problems on this side. One home was in the draw, one home was on a fairly flat open area at the top of the draw, and the other home was near the top of the deep canyon on the other side of the ridge. The dirt road into this area was narrow and the parking was minimal, so we had to limit traffic and vehicles. We had to determine where our escape route would be, because there was only one way in or out, and it was one vehicle wide. We found a wide grassy area near a pond large enough for us to sit tight with our engines if the fire blew over. The pond could supply water for two of the homes and give us a place to refill the engines.

The home above the pond was in good shape with plenty of open space. The owner planned to stay as long as possible to help keep his place wet. Not only did he have a great defensible place, he also owned an ice cream business and gave us all ice cream cones!

I had part of the crew run a hose lay from the pond to the home in the draw which was going to be the worst one to defend. The owners were an older couple. We cleared what we could away from the house and wet things down. The last house we visited required some work, as branches overhung the barn, which was close enough to the house to cause problems if the barn caught fire. This home was not as threatened as the others, so we postponed the work until we had the other homes taken care of.

The hotshot crew we had worked with the day before showed up and helped us. A dozer arrived to work a fireline into the canyon, trying to use an old existing road down in the canyon as part of the fireline, with the hotshots cleaning up the old road and building hand lines as necessary. Airtankers and helicopters were assigned to pretreat the area that the hotshot crew was working in. Once the line was in, the plan was to set a backfire from the fireline to meet the oncoming fire. While watching the dozer working on the steep slope, we all commented on the dozer operator, thinking he was either very very good or very crazy for the places he was putting that dozer into. We heard on the radio, about two hours later, that he had flipped his dozer and had been badly injured.

The superintendent of the hotshot crew had a four-wheeler so she could quickly move between her split crew. With our engines at the house on the ridge as kind of an informal staging area, she would drive in to check in with us and part of her crew every so often. She was the contact person for the aviation resources in this area, so we got to hear what was going on in the air. At one point a twin-engine leadplane flew over us and warned that an airtanker was inbound. We moved out of the way and had front-row seats to watch the airtanker drop. The propeller wash threw some retardant back at us and splattered the house. The owner and a couple members of his construction crew washed off the splattered retardant before it caused problems. The hotshot superintendent watched the drop and started cussing; she could see it was way off the mark they'd planned. Because the retardant was inside the area they planned to burn out, the burn operation had to be scuttled and a new plan put together quickly.

On the other side of the ridge, the fire was working its way up the draw and getting closer to the home of the older couple. We tried to get them to leave for town, but they refused. We kept checking on the place, keeping it wet as best we could, and finally called the sheriff in to see if he could get the couple to leave. Even he was unsuccessful. Soon the fire was close enough to the house that the hotshot superintendent ordered retardant drops near the house; we watched SEATs make numerous drops between the house and the fire.

A number of helicopter water drops were also made in the draw, trying to keep the fire from spreading. Not long after, we noticed the older couple's pickup heading up the narrow driveway away from their house. As they drove by our location, we saw that the white pickup was no longer white, but splashed pink – and not just a little bit. The cab was nearly solid pink and the couple had had to wipe the windows to see out. They stopped and told us they were heading into town to wash the pickup before the retardant dried. I didn't offer to have one of the engines wash their pickup for them.

As evening came on, the fire laid down a bit, and we switched crews for the night watch.

When we switched crews again in the early morning, things were looking better around the homes. We were provided another engine to help, and we had it set up at the pond so we didn't have to keep moving our attack engine. The hotshot crew was making good progress in the canyon, and another crew was finishing up the fireline in the draw. The fire was burning into the canyon, trying to make runs up the side toward us, but helicopter water drops on these fingers of fire knocked them down. The hotshot superintendent told us they were moving into a different area of the fire. She laughed as she told us her crew had given her a present that day – a gear shift they had found near one of the buildings. I had wondered why she never backed up her four-wheeler – she always went forward. Her crew had found out she couldn't get the darn thing into reverse, so had jokingly given her a gear shift with reverse prominently displayed on it!

The next day at the morning briefing, we heard that the effort was being switched to the fire across the river canyon, which was on the national forest. This fire, which had jumped the river two days ago, had been largely ignored while efforts were focused on protecting homes. Now, the threat to the homes was removed or diminished, and there were enough resources on the fire to work both sides of the canyon. I asked the incident commander if we could be released, and he agreed. I radioed the chief to bring everybody into fire camp. Most of the volunteers had never been in a fire camp before; they were able to clean up, eat breakfast, and talk with a few of the other firefighters. There was a good hour of paperwork left to do. So, the fire chief sent everyone else home, while we finished up the demob process.

The Blackerby Fire burned some 5,000 acres and cost $5 million to suppress – $3.1 million in just the first week. No structures were lost, and it was a good wake-up call to area residents.

Seven Devils and Combines

Back at home, my daughter Carmen took my camera and unloaded photos from the Sheep Fire, while I washed up and sat down for dinner. I told Cindy and Carmen what had happened at the fire, and with the photos, they could see what I was explaining. I was about ready for a shower when dispatch called out Salmon River to return to the subdivision. Wondering who had let the fire get away, I put my boots back on, kissed the girls goodbye, and headed back to the fire. On the way I thought about some of our toughest fires.

It doesn't happen often that either the Salmon River Rural Fire Department or Grangeville Fire Department would have two fires at the same time, but in the summer of 2006 Grangeville was requested for three fires at the same time. Grangeville Fire Department had been dispatched to a garage fire in town. Just as we got the fire knocked down and were ready to mop up, Grangeville Rural was dispatched to a lightning fire on the far north end of the district. Because all our firefighters were on this garage fire, the chief asked me to take the attack engine to the lightning fire. Two firefighters who were good at wildland firefighting came with me. We'd had light rain with the passing thunderstorm, so we held the other rural engine at the station, until we could see what this fire was all about. On our way there, Grangeville Fire was called out to a third fire, in a tree struck by lighting. This wasn't far from the garage fire, so an engine crew took off from the garage fire to put out the fire in the tree. We got to the lightning fire and found that local residents had already knocked the fire down, so we patrolled the area on the way back to town, looking for other lightning fires.

One summer night, I was staying at the family place

outside of Riggins, when a lightning storm came through and started a few fires. I was listening to radio traffic and heard dispatch call out Salmon River to help the Forest Service with a fire in the Seven Devils area. I drove to the nearest fire station, at Rapid River, where I could see the glow of the fire high on the ridge overlooking Rapid River. When the other volunteers arrived, the chief sent out an engine and a water tender. The driver of the water tender was not familiar with the area, so I rode shotgun with him. While heading up the gravel road, climbing the hill toward the Seven Devils, I noticed what I initially thought were burning embers coming down around us – but it was just wind-blown branches and needles reflecting the red from the warning light on top of the water tender!

We got to the first fire and put a line around it. Then, we moved up the road to the main fire to join up with the Forest Service on top of the saddle. The initial incident commander, a good friend of mine and fellow volunteer with the Grangeville Fire Department, had just come back from a recon of the fire. He told me the fire was at least 200 acres already. They were just going to stay parked at the saddle where it was safe and wait for daylight and reinforcements. He wanted to keep the water tender for now, so I went back down the hill with the engine. We reworked the lower fire on our way back to the fire station.

There were two other lightning-caused fires in the area burning briskly, so the Forest Service brought in an incident management team and more reinforcements. The main fire was poised on the ridge dividing the Snake River from the Salmon River. Numerous canyons had their start at this location, and a couple of these canyons headed toward Riggins and quite a few homes. I decided to meet with the new fire team as they were setting up, introducing the Salmon River department and asking about their strategy for structure protection. They hired us for structure protection, in case the fire moved into the Papoose and Squaw Creek drainages and for fire protection at the large helibase they'd established.

The helibase, set up in a large hay field with short stubble and flat ground, was a good site as long as the dust was kept down. The owner had cut the stubble as close to the ground as he could, and our job was to keep a water tender and an engine on site in case of a helicopter crash or fuel spill. We also used the tender to haul water to wet down landing spots to keep the dust and blowing weeds to a minimum. The crew was kept busy, as there were between four and six helicopters using the base.

One day a Sikorsky Skycrane – a heavy Type 1 helicopter – came in for the first time, and we wet down an area for it to land. The Skycrane has a tremendous prop wash, caused by its 72-foot rotor blade. We dumped 4,000 gallons of water on the landing area, but the area was still too dusty. The pilot flew over and dipped a load of water out of the river, (these heavy helicopters carry over 2,500 gallons of water) and spread it at the helispot, far more quickly than we could, and then landed. Even with all the water, the dust and blowing debris was tremendous. As soon as the helicopter shut down, we helped the pilot and crew hose down the engine intakes; they wanted to make sure the engines were clear of the dust and weeds blown up from the landing. This went on for three weeks, before the fires were contained.

Before the year was over, we would be involved in an interesting night fire. I had just gone to sleep the night of November 11, when my pager went off. The dispatcher said we had a brush fire south of town. On the way to the station I am thinking, "Yeah right, brush fire at night in November." It had to be a false alarm, or at least a controlled brush pile burn, as we'd had a couple of those already. The first three of us arrived at the station at the same time, grabbed our gear, and headed out in the attack engine. After notifying dispatch that Engine 1 was responding with three on board, we headed out of town looking toward the location of the reported fire. There was no fire in the vicinity of the reported location, so we continued driving. When we rounded the curve past the golf course, we saw a large glow on White Bird hill. We radioed the chief and Engine 2, letting them know the actual location of this fire. We arrived and could see the head of the fire coming at us, with a strong wind pushing it toward two homes and the main highway. We started working on the home closest to the fire, clearing burnable stuff from around it. Engine 2 was positioned along the highway in front of the next house.

We had finished with the first home when the chief asked if we could take the attack engine up the ridge to try to stop the fire there. We cut the fence and put the engine in 4-wheel drive. While I worked the nozzle, we attacked the head of the fire. We hit the head just as it was poised to jump the highway toward the other house, then worked the flank that was moving toward the first house. By this time, two state wildland engines arrived, one to assist us while the other went to the top of the fire where it had started. The wind died down, and the fire calmed down to just numerous pockets of orange flame. Once we had it knocked down enough so it didn't threaten the homes, the state released Engine 2 and asked if I could keep Engine 1 and my crew on the fire to help mop up. We were sent up to the top near the fire's origin, and we worked on putting out the larger flames along the edge of the fire. We used water sparingly, covering quite a bit of ground, but we ran out and had to head to town to refill the tank. Because the worst of the problems had been taken care of, the incident commander released us to return to the station. He had additional federal and state crews coming in at daylight to finish the job.

The funny part of this fire was that it was started by the Idaho Department of Lands to burn up slash piles from an earlier logging operation. During the day when they lit the piles, there had been no wind, but about 10:30 p.m. a strong wind had hit the piles and blew burning debris into the dry grass and brush. The fire, called the Old 95 Slop, was stopped at 110 acres.

We don't have many hazmat incidents in our area, but the potential is there. Because the Grangeville area is an agricultural hub, there are thousands of gallons of anhydrous ammonia fertilizer stored in the area. Late one cold spring night, we got a call about a possible fire at one of the agricultural supply facilities. I responded directly and met one of the police officers. We quickly drove around the facility and found a white vapor cloud coming from one of the company's tanker trucks. We didn't have a fire, but we did have a potentially dangerous situation.

While the police officer was filling in the dispatcher, I instructed incoming fire personnel. Both the police officer and I were a good distance away from the vapor cloud, but the wind shifted. We were soon hit with a strong odor of ammonia that took our breath away. Our eyes were watering and we couldn't breathe at all. We both moved around trying to get out of the vapor so we could breathe. The dispatcher kept telling the police officer to get out of there. We were finally able to move out of the vapor, and suck in some precious air. In a few minutes, the two fire engines arrived. A couple of firefighters put on their SCBAs; one of the arriving firefighters was a farmer and quite familiar with anhydrous ammonia. He wanted to go right in and turn off the valves, but I was reluctant to send him in without protection. One of the company employees arrived, and with a ready team backup, I let the two of them go in. They worked around the vapor cloud and quickly shut off the valve. In a short time the vapor cloud had dissipated; we left the situation to the owners.

The summer of 2007 was the summer for combine fires. Camas Prairie is a large area of mostly private agricultural land between the Salmon River and Clearwater River drainages, known for its production of wheat, rapeseed, grass, and lentils. Usually by mid-August, the combine harvesters are out cutting the wheat, harvesting the grain and leaving the straw and chaff in the fields. The first combine fire that year was a few miles outside of the district, and the fire burned through a field of wheat and into a canyon. Crews from the Cottonwood Rural Fire Department, the State of Idaho, and the Forest Service stopped the fire from getting established in the steep canyon.

A week or two later, Grangeville Rural got a call for a combine fire just north of town. When I arrived on scene, I had fire in front of me with flames taller than my Subaru on both sides of the road. I couldn't stay where I was – the fire was moving in my direction – so I drove through the tunnel of fire, turned around, and parked at a safe location.

The chief arrived with both Grangeville Rural engines, and he took over on the south side of the fire. I took charge of the north side where local farmers were arriving to help, coming in from the side road. Coordinating with the chief, I sent a tractor to plow around on the west side, then had a farmer's water truck set up to refill some of the local pickup trucks hauling small tanks of water.

One of our volunteers is a farmer and had told us numerous times that if a farmer shows up with a tractor and plow, get out of his way and let him work. I pointed out where I wanted the tractor plow to go, and the farmer took off. In a short time, he had the west head of the fire stopped against his plow line. A Forest Service engine showed up; the crew noticed the fire engines rushing by and the column of smoke. They headed out to see if they could be of assistance.

Once the wheat field fire was knocked down, we attended to the combine, which by now was just a metal hulk, steaming and surrounded by black. The operator knew he should have had his tractor plow close by, but he was eager to get the wheat harvested and had left the plow at the last field a few miles away.

Poe Cabin

Once I had radio communications with Salmon River Engine 3, we agreed to meet at the State Highway Department complex across from the subdivision. Engine 3 picked me up, and we headed up the hill into the Twilegar Subdivision. Fire had somehow jumped the subdivision road, and was burning between the highway and the homes. We were assigned a home to protect, while the other engine was assigned to the house across the draw.

The fire was down in the draw, where it was hard to get to, so the initial plan was to burn out the draw. I had our engine positioned between the draw and the home, and was just laying out hose when a Forest Service person snapped at me about blocking access for other smaller engines. I snapped back, pointing out the more-than-adequate distance we'd left all around us for equipment to get by.

An hour later, plans were changed; instead of burning out the draw, a small crew went with one of our hoses into the draw to put the fire out. After an hour or two, the fire was nearly out and our engine was released.

We were told to make sure we had eight hours of rest before returning to the fire camp for the next work shift, which meant we were not to make the 6 a.m. briefing. The division supe made sure we understood the work-rest guidelines, and that we would abide by them. It took me a while, but then, I realized that he was the same person I'd had words with earlier. Oops!

We radioed all of our volunteers on the fire to let them know of the discussion with the division supe, then we headed home.

In the morning, I arrived at fire camp for our assignment and found that after we had been released earlier that morning, plans had changed again. They did burn out the draw, and kept Engine 5 there for protection. So that crew got only a few hours of rest and were angry with us for being "late" to the fire assignment. We on Engine 3 were not happy that we'd missed out on the burn, and were now being criticized for following instructions. This certainly wasn't the first fire I had been on a fire with jumbled communications.

The second largest fire I had ever been on, occurred during the summer of 2007. I was working in Riggins, on a Friday afternoon, when Cindy, who was working in the office, mentioned that someone had called while I was in town getting the mail. The caller, from the White Bird area, had said he needed the rural fire department to help him. He said he was up Deer Creek and a fire was threatening his place, that he had plenty of water, but he needed help as soon as possible. Cindy was frantic because the man could not get help from the Sheriff's dispatch nor from the Forest Service. Cindy was not able to contact anyone on the SRRFD. As soon as I got back from the post office, Cindy explained the situation. This was weird, because we should have received a radio call dispatching the Salmon River department on this call. Fortunately, I was able to get hold of the fire chief and told him about the phone call. The chief told me that we were having to wait for the Forest Service request. Damn red tape and paperwork.

He explained what he knew of the fire, which had started the day before on the Snake River side of the ridge above the Deer Creek area. The Forest Service had called the Salmon River fire chief and asked him to send an engine to protect structures in case the fire jumped the ridge. By that night the fire had burned some 4,000 acres, but had stayed on the Snake River side. There was no use for the Salmon River engine, so they had returned to their station late that night.

So, now we get this frantic phone call that a home is threatened on our side of the ridge. The fire chief was waiting for the Forest Service to call, so we had to wait. I looked out to the north and saw – from 30 miles away – a huge column of smoke rising and then laying over to the east. This was not good at all. I didn't like waiting, so I called the interagency dispatch office and asked them about dispatching the SRRFD to the fire. The interagency dispatcher said the fire was in Deer Creek and that everyone was being evacuated. We needed to stay away for now, also, because a new incident management team was transitioning in, a decision would be a while in coming.

I called the chief back, but he was out. I told the captain to get ready to respond. He called a couple of firefighters to put them on alert. About twenty minutes later, I called interagency dispatch again and asked if they could dispatch us for structure protection. They said they had evacuated even the firefighting forces, and that the only engine they had left in the area was Forest Service Engine 13 – and they hadn't heard from them yet. I told dispatch we could assist Engine 13, if they were in trouble. Fire dispatch finally agreed and told us to meet at the Slate Creek Ranger Station. I then called dispatch at the sheriff's office and asked them to page the Salmon River department for the fire at Deer Creek.

The captain picked me up, and we drove with red lights and siren to the Slate Creek Ranger Station, where we ran into chaos and confusion. Engine 13 had just made it back from the fire, and its foreman was presenting a report. Everyone was waiting for orders from the new incident management team. Because no one knew what to do next, we were asked to stage along the Deer Creek road and wait for an assignment.

I'd been fighting fire long enough to know that one of the worst things firefighters can do is what's called "freelancing," or jumping in without a plan and without coordination or communication from other units on the fire. But, when I was just sitting there, and watching a huge cloud of smoke billowing overhead, knowing that a raging fire is probably eating up homes that we may have been able to save, the frustration was high. With my three engines and two water tenders just parked within four miles of the fire, we could not do a darn thing. But, I had no idea of what the fire was doing, where it was burning, or whether there was anyone in the fire area besides us. So we waited impatiently.

Finally a pickup pulled in to our parking area. The driver walked over and started yelling at us. He'd lost six buildings in the fire, which was the first we'd heard of any structures being lost. We were afraid there were going to be many more. He was raging at us about why we weren't helping, why we were just sitting on our asses. I expressed our sympathy, shared in some of his frustration, and told him we were waiting for orders. Because he was wanting to tear somebody apart, I gave him the only phone number I knew for the Forest Service. He finally marched off after threatening to sue everybody.

A short time later, a Forest Service employee stopped and introduced himself as part of the new team taking over management of this fire. He was gathering information on personnel and equipment already on the fire. While we were finishing up the paperwork, the incident commander arrived. He said he had an assignment for us, and that we should tie in with the division supe at the Robinson/Stowers Ranch about five miles up the Deer Creek road.

The first three miles of the road was mostly uphill, so we couldn't see the fire. From the top of the first ridge we could see over the canyon into the Deer Creek area, where we saw some of the fire. As we approached the second ridge, we drove along the fire's edge where it stopped along the road. We followed the road into the Deer Creek canyon itself and noticed the fire was still on our right side. When we got to the ranch we found White Bird Fire Department protecting a couple of outbuildings from the encroaching fire. We found the division superintendent and were assigned to check and protect all the homes from this point to the top of the saddle. The White Bird chief quickly briefed me on the situation with the homes we were to work on, then he headed to another threatened structure. I split the crew up, with an engine and water tender to stay at the ranch, protecting those buildings, and I took off with the other engine and tender to check the homes up the road.

About 500 feet past the ranch house, we ran into fire on both sides of the road. By now it was getting dark, with smoke so thick that the headlights worked only out to about 30 feet, or less. As we started to climb, we could see piles of burning debris, like slash piles or hay piles, on either side of the road.

We came to the driveway of the home that the White Bird chief had warned us about – he'd said they'd had to fight fire in the garage. I had the tender and engine stage in a wide spot near the driveway entrance, and I walked up the driveway. Kicking rocks and burning debris out of the road, I heard a vehicle and finally saw headlights coming through the smoke from the direction of the house. The driver pulled over to talk; it was the local lineman for the power company, checking on the services and system damage. Once the line truck reached the main road, I radioed the engine to come up carefully. We made it to the house and garage. The property was open, a prime example of defensible space. We walked around the house and took a quick check inside to make sure we couldn't see flames or fresh smoke.

The house seemed secure, so we checked the garage. It was metal-sided, but we saw a black streak near the middle of one side. We got inside and shined flashlights around; apparently, outside of the garage there had been a pile of scrap wood near the garage foundation. Embers had landed in the pile and caught it on fire. The fire had breached through a joint in the metal siding and ignited the plastic covering of the wall insulation. It then traveled up the wall and across the insulated ceiling. A piece of the burning plastic had dropped onto the canvas roof of a jet boat stored in the garage, and started the canvas on fire.

The White Bird engine had pulled up and opened the garage and knocked down the interior fire just as the canvas roof of the boat had started burning. We checked the inside, which was cool, and then checked the outside. We found a deep-seated fire burning some plywood that was partially buried under the cement foundation. We pumped water on it to cool it down, then moved on to the next home.

We were shocked to find the owner at the house. He asked us why we hadn't been there earlier when he'd called for help hours ago – he was the one who had called my work number hours before. I explained the situation and walked with him around the house, checking on the place while he explained his efforts in protecting his property. We could see he'd been proactive in keeping his place defensible.

He invited us into the house and told us that he'd called dispatch office to ask for the Salmon River department because a raging fire was approaching his place. The sheriff's dispatcher, though, didn't call us, because dispatching for this fire was being handled by the interagency dispatch office. He'd then found my office number and called, which is when I first learned of the fire. Not long after his call, a Forest Service engine crew stopped and told him to evacuate immediately. The owner sent his wife out with a small load of important items, and he was finishing up a few last chores before he, too ,was going to leave. However, the fire hit before he could get out, and he was trapped on his own property. He was better prepared then many homeowners, with a large generator to keep his water system working. He had been wetting down his property close to the house. When the fire hit, he sat down in his green lawn away from the trees and held the hose above his head showering water on himself. He survived without injury as the fire roared past his place. He had been the proud owner of some 550 fir and pine trees on his property, but they were now just blackened sticks.

We radioed the sheriff's dispatch to contact the owner's wife in White Bird to let her know her husband was safe, then we drove up the road to the next home.

We caught up with a Forest Service engine crew that was trying to burn ground fuels around the home. The fire had rushed down the draw on the east side, but had not yet burned down into the draw on the west side. A big unburned chunk of trees surrounded the house. The Forest Service crew did not need our help, so, we headed back down the road toward the our staging area at the ranch. We met with the rest of the Salmon River crew and ate a late dinner. A water tender and engine stayed at the ranch, while I sent the other engine and tender back up the road to recheck all the homes up there. We'd bypassed a couple of homes on our first rounds, so we split up – I went with one of the water tenders and checked on these other homes. The owner of one of these homes was checking on his place. He told us he had been on his property earlier, as the fire was roaring toward his place. He'd scraped away pine needles and weeds from against his house, then lit a backfire to burn out the fuels around the house. After he made sure his place was as protected as it was going to get, he drove across the road to a neighbors' and helped with protecting their place. These homes had been worked on over the past three years, abiding by the defensible guidelines provided by the local Forest Service fire prevention officer. After we checked these homes, we leapfrogged the engine crew and headed to the last home, where we had tied in earlier with the Forest Service engine crew.

By this time the Forest Service engine had moved on to another area, so we checked around while waiting for our engine crew. When they drove up to join us, they had quite the story. Coming up the road from the last home they'd checked, driving slowly in the thick smoke, a fawn had jumped out in front of them. It ran ten or fifteen feet, and collapsed. One of the crew got out to check on the fawn, and found that it had died, probably from seared lungs. As he was walking back to the engine, he spied a dead doe about twenty feet away lying in the borrow pit alongside the road. From what we learned later, in this area there were numerous burned animals, including a bear. The fire had hit so quickly that these creatures were caught. Most probably died of seared lungs while trying to escape.

It was after 3 a.m., and the fire had died down in most places. We could hear trees crashing every once in awhile, but otherwise the early morning was still and dark. As dawn painted the eastern sky, the night operations superintendent caught up with us. We were to continue with what we were doing until the day crew showed up to relieve us.

It was about 6 a.m. when we headed down the road toward the ranch staging area; in the daylight we could see much more of the damage. As we swung around one of the curves and looked below us, we saw a spread-out pile of metal roofing. We stopped for a better look, and saw a few more similar piles. Damn, those were the structures belonging to the angry man who'd told us he had lost everything. As we followed the road, we drove alongside one of the smoldering piles and realized that what we had thought were slash or hay piles burning, were actually what was left of his buildings.

We met up with the day crew at the staging area, and after briefing them we were released from the fire with instructions to return later in the afternoon for night duty. We parked a couple of the engines at the fire camp, then we all went home to clean up and sleep.

That afternoon, I arrived at the fire camp, checked around and waited for the rest of our crew and vehicles. I found out the fire had jumped to 20,000 acres, burning 16,000 in the afternoon blowup the day before. The fire camp was a work in progress, with sections still not set up, so we had to drive a mile to the ranger station for check-in. We found the night operations superintendent, and followed him to a café for dinner. He'd been told there were twenty people to be fed for the night shift, so the owner of the café had cooked twenty dinners. There were six of us plus the superintendent, but nobody else came. Later, we found out that the fire camp kitchen had just opened, and the rest of the night crews ate there. We didn't get the word. So, we ate and grabbed a couple extra dinners, with the café owner telling us to take more, it's just going to be thrown out.

We worked structure protection on a different section of the fire that night; we had two engines and one water tender. Our job was to patrol the main road, making sure homes were safe, and that the fire didn't jump the road. Because it was still daylight when we arrived at the new staging area, we did a quick drive-through of the homes in our area to get familiar with what we had and where they were. As it got dark, we took turns with the engines, one going up the road and one going down the road, checking on the homes and the fire. We had one place that was worrisome, so we spent a little more time there doing some preparation work. At our disposal was a local rancher and his small dozer, just in case things started moving during the night. It was a fairly quiet night, and we were relieved at daylight, again with instructions to return for the night shift.

By the late afternoon the fire camp was fully functioning. After we were briefed, fed, and given sack lunches, we headed back to the same location as the night before. Once there, though, we found out we were supposed to be on the day crew instead of the night crew. Another missed communication! We did one more check of homes in the area. We were released at midnight to return in the morning for the briefing and breakfast.

Our assignment that day started out the same – protect homes, but be available for initial attack on new fires. We had a larger area to work, and I had to send one of the engines to set up at a threatened home some distance off the main road. I then staged with my water tender at the same location from the previous night. We now had the local road department's 3,500-gallon water tender parked at our staging area. In between runs to check on homes, we refilled the smaller engines that were running around working the fire. Shortly after lunch, my tender was tasked with supporting an operation farther down the road, in a canyon called Sotin Creek, where the fire was becoming active and threatening to move into a subdivision.

The fire was waking up in the early afternoon, and had

already jumped a couple of firelines. This Sotin Creek area was a big problem, because if firefighters could not stop the fire at the ridge of this timbered canyon, it would burn into a large subdivision. I was able to listen in on the radio traffic since we were part of this division. I especially wanted to hear what was transpiring, since I had a water tender and two crew members involved directly with this part of the fire.

The plan was to get a hotshot crew onto the ridge, build a fireline, and get a few small wildland engines into the area to support the crew. Our tender was there to refill small engines when needed, but the fire decided it was not going to wait for all this to happen. It hit the ridge before any ground forces could get there. Air attack was ordered, with helicopters and airtankers dropping along the ridge and on the fire itself.

The leadplane pilot repeated, "We need boots on the ground now, or we are wasting the drops." The response was to continue hitting the ridge with everything, that ground forces have been delayed but are on the way. The pilots slowed the flames enough for the hotshots and a couple of engines to get in. The hot shot crew punched in a line that held. We were later told that the afternoon's air operations had cost over $250,000.

The northward movement of the fire was basically stopped, but it continued moving to the south away from the homes. I was able to leave the fire and spend a couple days catching up with my job. That's the problem with being a volunteer – your "real" job suffers while you are out trying to save lives and property.

A few days later the fire advanced toward another area of scattered homes. SRRFD had two engines working there, but our water tender was working in a different area. The fire was not yet a direct threat to the homes. So we were working to keep it from jumping the road and away from a set of corrals. The day before, part of the crew was protecting a cabin near these corrals, and during the night the fire had burned up to the edge of the corrals. In the beat-down grass within the corrals, a hotshot crew had their two crew trucks parked, so we made sure to keep the fire from burning in there and threatening the vehicles.

In the early afternoon, the division supe told me to send an engine to help with a spot fire threatening to jump the road a half mile or so from our position. I took Engine 4 there. We ran hose and helped the hand crew and a small engine hit the spot fire just as it reached the road. Both engines had arrived in the nick of time. Our engine, with a 1,000-gallon tank, supplied water for the crew building fireline, and a portable water tank was also set up with a large water tender to re-fill it. Our engine then pumped water out of the tank and to the fire crew. We later installed a portable water pump to replace our engine, freeing us up to either bring more water or be ready to roll.

That evening, we were called back to the corrals where we met up with our other engine crew. The hotshot crew and another small engine were there, all milling around waiting for something to happen. We were kept in the dark for a while, then the hotshots moved their vehicles out of the corrals and lit the grass in the corrals on fire. Our task force leader told us the division superintendent wanted to burn out the long stretch of road from the corrals up to the saddle at the ridge top where the roads met.

We were to follow behind the firefighters, helping them when they needed water. All our work that day protecting the area around the corrals now seemed for naught. A local rancher showed up and told me he had cows in the draw between the main fire and this burnout; he hadn't been warned and there was now no way to move those cows. We were just sick and angry. I understood the strategy of the burnout, but I could not understand the seemingly uncaring attitude regarding the rancher's cows.

With the burnout under way, we followed behind with our engines checking for spot fires and putting out fires in trees. It was well past dark when we finished, and we were all sent to a spike camp just a couple miles away. By 4:30 a.m. breakfast had been sent up from the main camp, so we dished up and sat down under some generator-driven lights. The task force leader and I had a long chat over breakfast. He admitted that the frustration last night had gotten to him, and he wasn't happy about the cows and the way the burnout had been handled.

That day, we supported water needs of fire crews in the area, and in the early afternoon, we were working on a wide ridge with a good view west across the Snake River/Hells Canyon into Oregon. We saw a large fire burning directly across from our fire. Our fire was moving up river on the Idaho side of the canyon while the Battle Ridge Fire on the Oregon side was moving down river.

Once again, the threat to structures was abated, so I checked out of the fire that night and went home to get back to my job. One engine was kept on the fire for another week or two until the fire was contained. The Poe Cabin Fire burned nearly 60,000 acres, severely injured three firefighters, burned seven structures, and cost over $15 million.

Parsonage and Gas Station

About 9a.m,. I met up with Engine 3 at the fire camp, where we received our instructions, and headed to John Day Creek to protect structures. We'd learned that the fire on Sunday had grown from 1,600 acres to just under 16,000 acres.

Salmon River Engine 5 and one of the water tenders took up positions at the house where the fire had been stopped the day before. A dozer line had been built around the house, and the field and hillsides to the east and north had been burned. The danger was the south and west sides, with a stand of trees that had not yet burned. Engine 3 and the other water tender took up positions at a junction about a mile downstream from Engine 5, which gave us the ability to roll in any of three directions. We had two water pumps in the creek at our location, so we were looking good for water.

Not long after setting up at this junction, I was scouting the area and saw flames coming up to the ridge from the other side. We hadn't realized the fire was that close. The structure protection supe had just arrived as the fire started backing down the hill toward us. He sent a small engine to help us, and asked us to wet down the power poles between us and the fire. We agreed on an emergency plan and possible evacuation of our personnel and equipment if the fire should get out of hand.

The Type 6 engine helping us was from Montana. Being smaller and carrying less water, it could move around faster than our big Type 2 engine. The engine foreman, also the owner, told us that she had worked many extra hours as a waitress and doing health care work to pay for her engine. This year, she was making good money, working fires around the country and living what some people only dream of.

While waiting for the fire moving toward us, I remembered a few past fires that had become nightmares.

One day in the middle of summer, I was driving up Seven Devils road outside Riggins to pick up a computer from a customer. I saw smoke from the general area of where I was going, and thought it strange that somebody would be chancing a controlled burn this time of year. As I turned at the junction of Squaw Creek and Seven Devils roads, I saw that the fire was coming from the shop where I was to pick up the computer. Both a Riggins engine and a Salmon River engine were working the fire. The rest of the story is best told by the owner in his own words:

"As I sat on the hill, watching my shop burn and the dozen or so firemen frantically try to save what they could, I looked down the road and saw John Sangster of PCRCS Computer coming up the road to my house in his Subaru. John had been helping me the day before with my wireless internet at the shop and getting my new computer system up and running. I had offered my old system to him and he was coming to pick it up. I watched as he pulled into the scene and quickly got out. He frantically threw the back hatch open and started digging through his gear. I thought perhaps he was digging for a camera. Suddenly he pulls out his boots and fireman overalls, hops into them, and follows with the coat and helmet. In an instant he became another fireman in the fray. The last time I saw him that night he was on a ladder, opening the attic and dowsing the last of the flames."

~ Mark Hollon

From "Volunteers make a difference, people look after each other", The Current, September 2009 by Rachelle Barger.

Hollon's shop was heavily damaged, and the brand-new computer was melted. I left the older computer for him to use until he was able to get another new one.

A late-night page in November announced there was a house fire in the Grangeville Rural fire district. It was on my side of the district, so I radioed to dispatch that I was on my way. As I followed the gravel road around a curve and saw the red-orange glow of the house, I knew this was not going to be a quick fire. I pulled into the driveway and told dispatch the house was fully involved. Flames were roaring out of nearly every opening on the main floor. The other assistant chief, hearing my radio traffic, radioed for additional water supplies. I geared up and spoke with the sheriff's deputy to make sure everyone was out of the house.

The attack engine arrived, but a pickup truck and trailer were in the drive; we dragged them out of the way just as Engine 2 arrived. The owners were out of town, but one of the daughters and a friend had been in the basement. They'd heard a crash upstairs and had called the sheriff to report a possible burglary. The neighbors happened to look over to the house and saw flames. They called the girls to warn them, then reported the fire to dispatch. The crashing the girls had heard upstairs was things falling from shelves weakened by the fire. They had escaped over to the neighbors' place and called the parents.

We moved the attack engine to the back of the house and ran hose from Engine 2 to both the attack engine and the front of the house. One of the Grangeville City engines arrived to shuttle water, and a little later we were being supplied by a couple of tank trucks from a local agricultural warehouse.

This home was brand new, built with new technology using concrete poured into a foam block material instead of wood framing. This type of construction fought against us. We switched to a foaming operation since the application of just water was not letting us gain on the fire. Once we started foaming the fire, we were finally knocking it down. The concrete and foam core material, however, held the heat in each room – and anything burnable burned. Anything made of wood seemed to just vaporize.

While we were mopping up, we found many pockets of blue flame, indicating burning foam. The other assistant chief and I sent most of the crew home early in the morning. I stayed with another firefighter to finish mopping up and watch the place until the owners showed up. The sheriff came out, and when the owners arrived, we all walked around the house and explained what had happened.

When I left, the other assistant chief took over the day watch; he ordered in an excavator to rip into a corner of the kitchen where it joined the garage, as there was a stubborn fire burning in the rubble that we couldn't get to. After visiting with the insurance agent and the fire marshal, we learned that this new type of construction, the concrete and foam core, has been a serious problem for firefighters in other areas of the country.

After this house fire and the Blackerby Fire of 2005, the Grangeville Rural Fire District commissioners agreed to purchase a water tender, if I could find one that was affordable. My requirements were tough, and it took a long time to find one that matched.

The Galt Fire Department, just south of Sacramento, California, was selling their 4,000-gallon water tender for a reasonable price. Cindy and I drove to California to combine business with a family visit. I checked out the tender and its records and bought it. One of the Grangeville volunteers, experienced in operating heavy equipment on his farm, flew down to meet us. He and I took turns driving the tender home, with Cindy following us in the car. A FEMA grant helped us purchase a 3,000-gallon portable tank and a large portable water pump, which we mounted on the water tender.

Our first use of the tender came early the next year, on a cold winter night. We received a page for a house fire on Cove Road, near the far southeastern edge of our district. Both the chief and an assistant were headed to the fire in their own vehicles, so I stayed at the fire station with a small crew in case we got another fire call. It was a long drive on icy roads, so I sent the water tender to the fire without waiting for the chief to request it. The tender driver was a professional truck driver, so I figured he could handle the truck better than anyone else.

Fortunately, the only person who had been in the house was not injured. But, by the time he got out and drove to the neighbor's to report the fire, the house was fully involved. When the engines arrived, all the firefighters could do was keep the fire out of the nearby structures and equipment. Having the water tender there allowed the firefighters to put plenty of water on the fire, and not worry about needing another engine to come out with a load of water. Before getting the water tender, we would have needed about eight trips with one of the city engines to match the volume of water carried by the water tender.

Funeral and a wreck

After a five-year battle with cancer, Cindy's mother, Mary, lost the fight, and we gathered with family and friends for a burial at the Riggins cemetery. When the interment was finished, we all met at Cindy's parents' house on the Little Salmon River, for a celebration of Mary's life. In the middle of this get-together, I noticed a couple of sheriff's vehicles and two ambulances heading south on Highway 95, across the river from the house. I turned on my pager and heard something about a wreck not far away. Then, the extrication unit sped by. I decided to see what was going on. In this area, as in many areas across the country, volunteer EMTs and firefighters are dwindling in number, so it was a good chance that the EMTs would need all the help they could muster.

The wreck included two heavily damaged vehicles, EMTs yelling, bloodied people in pain, and mass confusion. I was wearing my turnout coat over my suit, and after a quick look around, walked over to what looked like the worst situation. One of the injured was still in the mashed vehicle, and the

EMTs were having a hard time trying to get him onto a backboard and out of the vehicle. I was able to step in and help with the muscle work, and we lifted him out.

Another victim was sitting on the ground staring, leaning up against a car. She was white as a ghost. There was no evident blood nor injuries, but she wouldn't respond to questions. I was afraid she was in shock, and after checking with one of the EMTs, I put my heavy fire coat over her shoulders and went back to help the EMTs.

The badly injured were loaded into the two Riggins ambulances, while two more ambulances arrived from New Meadows. The other injured persons walked or were carried to the ambulances. I retrieved my fire coat and returned to the celebration of a life, while tow trucks started removing the mess of the wreck.

The year 2009 ended with a roar, and 2010 began the same way. Right after Christmas, in the middle of the night, I got a call from a customer and good friend in Riggins. "We need you here in Riggins right now," she said. One of the parsonages was burning, and it could easily spread to the church or one of the nearby houses. I was 45 miles from this fire, but I figured I could relieve one of the volunteers by the time I got there. So, I headed toward Riggins, stopping at the Lucile fire station ten miles before Riggins to grab Salmon River Engine 4, in case they needed another structure engine. It took nearly an hour from the time I got the phone call, but I joined in with the rest of the Salmon River firefighters assisting the Riggins Fire Department on this blaze. The fire was knocked down by then, but a long ways from being out. I grabbed a hose and helped in mopping up the heavily damaged house.

The minister and his wife were visiting family out of town that night. It is always saddening to be there when residents return to find their home and belongings either gone or heavily damaged. While mopping up, you could see blackened piles of clothing still smoking, partially burnt books piled in a jumbled mess, globs of melted plastic items, and blackened walls and furniture, those that didn't burn up. When you look around inside a house and all you see is black covering everything, it just makes you sick – all that stuff underneath the black was someone's belongings. A few weeks later, I talked to the minister and he said even though they'd lost everything, he had found a few important items in drawers protected from the worst of the fire.

The firefighters who had fought this parsonage fire had been on a structure fire earlier in the day, at a house a mile outside of Riggins. The area had limited access, but with the help of the Riggins Fire Department, enough equipment and volunteers were rounded up to subdue the fire, but not before a lot of damage had been done. That was what mutual aid was all about – firefighters helping each other as best they could.

Two weeks later, I was in Riggins when my pager went off. I couldn't hear the dispatcher, so I called in. The dispatcher told me there was a fire at the gas station in White Bird, and the Salmon River department was needed. Taking Engine 3 from the Rapid River station, I headed north to White Bird. The concern was for the other buildings near the gas station, and even though I was 35 miles away, the engine might be needed.

The main entrance to White Bird off the highway was right in front of the gas station. I took the alternate route into White Bird, coming in from the south in case the gas station fire was blocking the entrance. White Bird Fire Department volunteers had kept the fire from spreading to the adjacent motel and telephone office, both very close to the gas station building that was on fire.

Salmon River's Engine 5 was positioned to protect buildings on the north side, and was supplying water from one of the town's hydrants. A couple of us volunteers took a hose and worked on what was left of the upstairs apartment.

The fuel pumps had been removed earlier, and no fire reached the underground tanks. There had been numerous explosions inside the building before we arrived, but thankfully the explosions had blown out toward the street instead of toward the other buildings. After a few hours of mopping up, we were released by White Bird to return to our stations.

During the summer, the region experienced lightning storms. A few fires were ignited even though the area was still green from the wet spring. One morning after a hammering thunderstorm, I heard Salmon River paged out to a fire outside of White Bird. From the location given, I was concerned that it was close to some homes, so I responded from Grangeville.

As I arrived, one of the volunteers said he had seen a car pull away just as he'd arrived. This seemed a weird place for a lightning strike, but a good place for a human-caused fire, so I investigated. The fire itself was very small, and within thirty feet of the Salmon River. After a quick sweep of the ground, I looked up at a nearby pine tree, and there it was – a chunk of bark missing.

Lightning strikes are usually found higher up, near ridge tops or in the taller trees. In this case, however, lightning had hit a tree near the river, at the lowest spot of the canyon, completely bypassing higher objects on the surrounding hills.

We had the fire out when the Salmon River engine arrived, and a short time later one of the Forest Service engines arrived to take over. The foreman for the Forest Service engine was briefed on what we'd done and what we'd found, and we headed home.

The wet spring had kept fire activity fairly low, but by the end of summer Grangeville got busy. We were called to a fire about three miles beyond the boundary on the far northeast corner of the district. The hot, dry weather conditions and the harvesting going on suggested to the fire chief that we had better deal with the fire at its source rather than wait for it to hit our district.

When we arrived, we found a trailer load of round hay bales burning, not too far from a field of grain. As we started attacking the fire, the owner of the load of hay came over to talk, and we both started laughing – he was the Forest Service engine foreman that I had met recently on the lightning fire in the Salmon River canyon. We shook hands and he said, "You saved my butt again." A state engine arrived and took over the fire, so we were released to return to Grangeville.

Wind-Driven Field Fire

I was taking photos of the flames burning slowly downhill toward us when another firefighter yelled. I worked my way back to see what he needed, and he told me that he and a couple others had seen four wolves on the ridge ahead of the flames. They didn't stick around long, he said, and had moved away from the approaching flames.

We had been watching the hillside for activity, when we heard a loud whoosh and saw thick black smoke just on the other side of the ridge to our left. Up until then, the fire had been to our right. Another loud whoosh, more black smoke, and then one of the crew yelled "Spot fire!"

Sure enough, a fire had started right near where I had just wet down a power pole. That spot had grown to twenty feet in a matter of seconds. More spot fires started popping up. I had one of my crew radio the engine and water tender up the road to bug out and get down here right away. The fast-moving spot fires reminded me of a wind-driven field fire a couple of years back.

The fairly quiet fire season of 2010 was not over. I was delivering a repaired laptop to a customer in town, and I noticed a large smoke column developing just to the west of the city limits. This time of year the field burning is heavy, with many plumes of brown smoke scattered around the huge prairie. This smoke column bothered me, though, because there was a brisk wind blowing out of the southwest. As I handed the laptop to the customer, dispatch paged out Grangeville Rural for a field fire threatening homes. Only a few blocks from the fire station, I arrived just as the attack engine was leaving. The fire chief was in the attack engine with two firefighters. The first assistant chief was unable to leave the city, which meant I could go ahead and respond as well. I ran to the 4,000-gallon water tender and fired up the big diesel. Letting it warm up, I put on my fire gear. Rural Engine 2 was rolling out the door, with three firefighters on board, as I waited for a second firefighter to go with me. The rest of the volunteers stayed in town to handle any fire response within the city.

We took off and headed west out of town; the firefighter with me radioed that we were en route. At the fire, I saw that both Grangeville Rural engines had left the highway and were out in the field hitting the southeast flank of the fire. I was more concerned with the homes threatened by the head of the fire, which we could not see from our location.

I drove toward the fire's head to get closer to the threatened homes. We topped over a rise that had us blocked from seeing the head of the fire, and all we could see was dark smoke, obscuring even the highway. We couldn't tell if the fire had jumped the highway up ahead, whether it had hit the homes, or where exactly the head of this fast-moving fire was.

Afraid to commit the big water tender to a situation where it could get stuck or trapped, I staged it near a couple of old buildings threatened by the east flank of the fire. We set the tender up to both protect the structures and refill engines. There were numerous small trucks belonging to the two agricultural supply businesses in town, each with a small tank of water and a pump, flitting around helping knock down the fire. The field was mostly stubble, but there was a section of uncut wheat and some areas of brush. From our vantage point, we could see the flame front advancing along the east flank, moving rapidly and belching out smoke. The smoke column was laid over nearly horizontal, so we couldn't see the head of the fire, and the threatened homes were right in the smoke column.

We soaked down the old buildings and filled one of the small trucks. Then, the state police officer escorting traffic asked us to move off the highway for fear we would get hit.

After repositioning the tender into a green area just off the highway, we filled another truck and laid out hose and started putting out some of the approaching fire. The wind was blowing around 25 to 30 miles per hour, and embers were going everywhere ahead of the fire, kindling new flames in the stubble. The wind also quickly dried up the water just applied.

A couple of State engines arrived along with an incident commander, who took over the fire operations. A couple of Forest Service engines showed up and worked the fire along the highway. The southwest wind was still blowing strong, but it began to turn as the cold front passed. Both Rural engines were out along the southern flank, dousing burning power poles.

The incident commander pulled up alongside the water tender and asked for both of the Rural engines right away – the fire had jumped the highway to the east and was threatening other homes. I radioed the chief and passed along the need for help, and soon the attack engine drove by heading for the slopover. Then Engine 2 arrived from working on the power poles, but had one flat tire and the second one going flat. While they were stopped alongside the road working on burning power poles, a clump of burning straw that had lodged between the rear dual tires on the passenger side burned enough to weaken the sidewalls of the outside tire and flattened it.

We called the local tire shop, then headed the tender toward the slopover. By this time, the attack engine needed water, so I drove the highway trying to find both it and a safe spot off the road to refill. I saw a couple of state and federal engines working the slopover ahead and on my right side, with the fire heading into a stand of brush and trees below a house. Trying to find a safe place to park, I glanced in my rearview mirror and saw that fire had jumped the highway behind me and was roaring across a field toward some trees. After I radioed to let the others know about the second slopover, the attack engine found me, and we filled them up.

The winds had changed and were coming more out of the west, so the fire was jumping on the east flank and spotting across the highway.

Rural Engine 2 had its tires fixed and rejoined the firefight. I moved the water tender to a safe area and refilled one of the small agricultural trucks. The driver of a pickup heading north on the highway slowed down and motioned to us, pointing to the south. I drove the tender back onto the highway and over the rise blocking our view, so we can see what the pickup truck driver was trying to tell us. We saw that the fire had turned and was now roaring toward a couple of homes and a trailer park. I radioed the chief, telling him of the situation, then found a wide driveway in which to park the tender. A Forest Service engine pulled up alongside us and we watched for spot fires across the highway, ready to jump on any smokes.

This field fire, now pushed by winds from the northwest, was munching up ground where some engines had been earlier. The winds were drying up any water we spread on the unburnt stubble, so the fire was headed back toward where it had started. We had only one spot fire jump the highway on the trailer park side, and the Forest Service crew was right there to knock it down. We had emptied the water tender by then, so we drove back to town and refilled.

On the way back, we had to fight the traffic of both sightseers and passersby. I felt sorry for the Deputy directing traffic at the intersection – he had a mess. We were trying to turn right off Highway 95 onto Highway 7 to get back to the fire. Others were trying to make a left onto Highway 7 from the opposite lane – plus there was a backup of traffic trying to turn onto Highway 95 from Highway 7. Just as the officer opened a spot for me to turn onto Highway 7, a sightseer pulled up into the opening and had everyone blocked again. Finally, I could see the slimmest of openings between stopped vehicles and decided to bull my way through. After motioning to the officer what I was going to do, I put the water tender in gear and drove through, without scraping any vehicles. I parked once again near the fire to refill trucks.

We had been on this fire for over six hours, when the winds finally died down and the fire stayed contained. Both Rural engines were released, but I was asked to keep the water tender on site to refill the few engines left mopping up and patrolling.

It was about 8 p.m., and the winds had been calm for an hour or more. The fire had laid down, and a farm tractor with disk was working part of the burned field, tilling in any still hot stuff into the dirt. This 1100 acre fire was now finally subdued.

The incident commander released the few remaining engines and our water tender, and told us all to get over to the restaurant for dinner before they closed up. The five Forest Service crew members and I were the only ones to head for dinner, where we had a great time sharing some past war stories.

Hungry Flames

The fire was scattered over two-thirds of the hillside now, spreading quickly. Engine 5 and the water tender pulled in from up the road. I sent them and our other water tender down the road to a safety zone in a field away from the fire. My plan was to get the slow-moving vehicles out before things got really bad. I kept the small engine with Engine 3, figuring we could fight our way out if necessary. Shortly, after the engine and both tenders left, the entire hillside was on fire, with pine and fir trees torching and sending out showers of embers.

The caretaker of one of the homes pulled up on his four-wheeler, and while talking with us, he looked over his shoulder and spied a spot fire. He yelled, and the crew of the small engine, which was closest, grabbed hose and took off running. The spot fire was across both the road and the creek, in thick brush and trees. Thanks to quick action, the spot fire was caught in time, and was the only one that crossed the creek. By dark, the fire had calmed down. We were released, replaced with a night patrol. On our way out of the fire, the adrenaline rush fading, I recalled other fires that had burned with mind-boggling flames.

About a month after the wind-driven field fire, we were called out in the middle of the night for a house fire. We could see the fire's glow from the station and knew it was going to be nasty. As we were heading out, one of the firefighters who lived across the street from the burning house drove up and yelled to respond with everything – the fire was big. When we got there, we saw a large house with a ferocious fire pouring out one end. We put on our gear, laid out hoses, and confirmed that no one was home. The engineer on Engine 2 fired up the water cannon and poured water onto the fire while we shot water into the windows trying to hit the fire.

The house was in three sections: main living area, kitchen and family area, and a garage with living area upstairs. The main living area was completely engulfed, so we tried to hit the fire with as much water as we could through the window and door openings. When we'd knocked it down a little, I led an interior attack team in through the kitchen and family area, working our way to the doorway into the main living section. As I moved into the burning section, one of my legs broke through the wooden floor. I managed to crawl out of the hole and then promptly crashed through another spot on the floor. I yelled a warning to the others to stay out of the this area. We were able to stop the interior spread at the doorway by spraying water onto the fire from the doorway.

While the hose team mopped up the main living area, I searched the upstairs over the garage. This area had no fire. Since there were no problems in this third section, we were able to concentrate on saving the middle section. There still was lots of fire to knock down.

While we were packing up, one of the firefighters noticed wafting smoke near the ridge of the roof where the main section and middle section roofs came together. A couple of firefighters got onto the roof and tore it up near the junction of the burned section. The crew found a pocket of fire that had been missed earlier and rooted it out and hosed it down. It was just coming daylight when we put the last piece of hose back on the engine. We were glad that only a third of the house was destroyed, and our hard efforts showed.

A week later, we were again awakened in the middle of the night, this time for a semi truck on fire at the Depot gas station. When we arrived, about 5 minutes after the call, the cab of the truck was fully involved. Luckily, the semi was parked far enough from the gas pumps that we didn't worry about the fire reaching them. We applied foam to the interior of the cab, and the fire was knocked down quickly.

A couple of us got into the cab to mop up, and one of the firefighters spied a black, round object under the bed in a pile of debris. The size and shape of what was visible chilled the few who saw it, and immediately the yell went out 'where's the driver?'. The truck driver/owner showed up, alongside the deputy he was talking with. The driver was asked if there had been anyone riding with him. No, he had been alone. The deputy was told what was found in the cab, and with permission, one of the firefighters removed the debris hiding the rest of the object. Thank heavens it was starting to look more like a bowling ball, and when asked, the driver confirmed that he always carried his favorite bowling ball. Whew, what a relief.

The driver was shirtless, for he had been asleep in the sleeper portion of the cab when he was awakened by the smell of smoke and strange popping noises. The fire was growing quickly, and he couldn't get back into the cab for his shirt and other items. He told us he was damn lucky he'd stopped where he did. If he had stopped alongside the highway somewhere else, he could have lost everything, including the load he was hauling.

A week later, we got a call for a fire at a restaurant. We had been there a few times before, for grease fires in the duct work above the stoves. It was just past midnight, Sunday morning. Thinking the bar side was still open, I expected trouble getting close to the fire with people and vehicles in the way. When we arrived, though, there was no one in sight. The place had closed early. We saw that the fire had already broken through on the south end between the main entrance overhang and the wall.

We had a large wooden building on fire, with a number of structures close by. The hospital was across the street to the north, the ambulance station at the end of the parking lot to the east, a gas station across the street to the west, and a large warehouse to the south to worry about. Plus, there was an apartment over the kitchen on the west side.

When the fire broke through, it got enough air inside the

restaurant that it flashed over inside – and soon we had nearly the entire building involved.

The restaurant was built to resemble a large ranch house, but with a large sunken dining area containing tables and chairs. The sunken dining area was surrounded by a raised dining area, split up by booths along three of the walls. The south side of the restaurant consisted of a large bar, also filled with tables and chairs. Outside the bar was a small metal shed full of cut apple wood, used to supply the large open fire spit. The entire pile of firewood was burning. Next to the shed was the propane gas line going into the restaurant and bar. It was leaking propane and feeding the fire. Once the propane was shut off, we put out the fire in the shed, while the rest of the crews worked on the restaurant itself.

There was an apartment/office upstairs on the west side that we were worried about. The second engine was set up on that side, trying to keep the fire from advancing any further into the kitchen and upstairs apartment.

We had two 2½-inch hose lines, the water cannon, and four 1½-inch hose lines set up around the fire. I wanted to set up one of the hoses at the main entrance and start an interior attack, but we couldn't send a crew inside until the roof finished falling in.

A short time later, after much of the roof had collapsed, the interior team started to move in. A drunk local guy walked right up to the interior team as they were starting in through the front door. A couple of us ran to intercept him, before he had stumbled into the building, and backed him away. A police officer finally escorted the guy away.

Once the fire had calmed down, we sent a team in to put out the burning debris in the bar. Another team worked upstairs in what was left of the apartment. Much of the roof had collapsed into the sunken dining room. However, where some of the roof was still standing, it was supporting some heavy machinery. This made working inside a serious challenge, trying to be careful not to jar the poorly supported roof sections holding the machinery. It took hours to mop up the interior. After some investigation, the fire was determined to be arson-caused.

Once in a while, the Grangeville Fire Department is provided an old house to practice on and then burn to the ground. Early in November, we were given an old house for training – the owners wanted to replace it with a new modular home.

There were serious concerns over the two houses on either side of the training house – one had vinyl siding but was a fair distance off, and the closer house had a wooden-sided garage. We set up Engine 2 with a line to the closest hydrant and ran attack lines to protect both adjacent homes. We also had two attack lines at the front of the house to cover an emergency while crews were inside.

We used a smoke machine to smoke up the interior of the house, and ran firefighter training sessions for about an hour. We had roof training exercises and opened a few holes in the roof with a chainsaw for ventilation practice, but we also used these for drawing fire up and out when we were finished with the exercises.

The training inside the house was designed to familiarize firefighters with the use of SCBAs, and with crawling around inside a building with zero visibility. After the training was finished, we started three fires in the old house in strategic locations to get the middle to burn first. During the fire build-up stage, we let firefighters inside to watch the fire expand.

The training and the fire went exactly as planned – until a change in the wind direction sucked a pocket of heat toward the vinyl-sided house and warped the siding. Of course, this made the local paper and stirred up a hornets' nest for a couple of weeks, but the training we put on for the crew was priceless.

Hours later, the pager woke me up with a call from dispatch about a fire. The address sounded really close to the house we'd just burned down. I was afraid this fire was caused by some embers from the burning we did earlier. We got there and found that the fire was a block away, and it was just a burned-up plastic trash can! Someone had put hot embers from a burned pile of leaves into their plastic trash can. Fortunately, they had set the trash can on the sidewalk instead of near the house. All we could do was to hose down the smoking pile of burnt plastic and trash. Luckily, it had nothing to do with the training fire we'd done earlier in the day!

Barn and Vehicles

My car was at the fire camp, so the engineer operating Engine 3 drove to the camp and dropped me off. He then headed Engine 3 back to Riggins for replenishment. We were asked to be at the camp in the morning for briefing, so I headed over the hill to Grangeville for a quick dinner, shower, and sleep. A few hours later, I woke up, grabbed some breakfast, and headed to the fire camp. On the way to the fire camp, I started thinking of some of the fires I had been on just the year before.

As usual, the new year had started off with chimney fires. Fortunately, most of the chimney fires we run into are entirely contained inside a good chimney, and there is no fear of the fire extending outside the chimney. However, we had one chimney fire in an old farmhouse that caused us some grief.

We were paged to a chimney fire just outside of town. Upon arrival we could see some dark colored smoke coming out of the chimney of the old farm house. The wind was blowing briskly, and the creosote in the old brick chimney was burning hot. We checked and could not find fire outside of the chimney. So we let the chimney cool down and left it to the owners to watch. A few hours later, we received a page, the dreaded call to return to a previous fire call.

No department ever likes receiving a call back to a fire they had finished working on. It means someone screwed up, something was missed, and we take it personally. We responded with both rural engines and sure enough, there was fire in the wall behind the wood-burning stove, and in the roof. While one crew was up removing part of the roof to get to the fire, three of us were in the attic trying to get to the seat of the fire. We finally found it and dug it out.

Putting the puzzle together, we found that the brick chimney was not lined, and a small hole in the old mortar cement allowed heat and flame to extend into the wood joist standing against the chimney. This was hidden by a section of two ceilings, one stacked on the other with a ¾ inch gap. The fire had been hiding in this gap earlier, and after smoldering awhile, the wind had caught the hidden flame, feeding it air. Fortunately, the owners were in the house, when the smoke alerted the owners that there was a problem.

It had been a few months since the last night fire, so when the page woke me up in the middle of the night, it took a second to register what the noise was. The dispatcher announced that Grangeville Rural Fire had a barn fire past Mt. Idaho. When I arrived at the fire station, I headed right to the water tender and fired it up, while the attack engine was headed out the door. While I was getting my fire gear on, Engine 2 headed out the door. I hopped in the water tender and while waiting for the air pressure to build up, I motioned for one other firefighter to hop in the truck. As soon as the air pressure alarm went off, I drove out the door and headed to the fire. On arrival, we positioned the tender so we could refill the engines as needed. The barn was a complete loss, so we spent some time just pulling metal roofing away from the pile of burning hay, restacking the metal in a safe spot.

While we worked on uncovering the burning hay, the owner told us that there had been a couple of lambs in the barn, her children's 4-H projects. Apparently, a heat lamp had been knocked over and had set the straw bedding on fire. The lambs didn't have a chance. After a few hours of moving the metal and spreading out the hay, we were able to return home.

In November, in the late evening, Grangeville Fire was called out to a structure fire. The owners had moved into a different house and were selling this one, so no one was in the house at the time of the fire. The neighbors had seen the fire as they were getting ready for bed, and had called it in. I was driving the attack engine and all three of us in the cab had misunderstood the address. After heading in the wrong direction for a few blocks, I realized my mistake. After a few turns and playing race car driver, we pulled into the fire just ahead of the second engine. When we arrived, the fire was just coming out of the kitchen window. We laid a quick hard line attack on the flames to knock them down, while some of the firefighters were getting their SCBAs on and operational.

One team advanced a hose line to the roof and the second team took a hose into the kitchen area, where the worst of the fire was. The heat and smoke damage was more extensive than the fire damage, which had melted light switches and warped light bulbs down the hall away from the kitchen. We had to tear up the kitchen sink area, and found what looked like the cause of the fire – an under-the-counter heater that had either shorted or overheated, and set the wood of the cupboard on fire.

The next night, we were paged out for a vehicle fire near the local automobile dealership. We found a pickup truck parked on the street with fire boiling out of the engine compartment and just starting to burn into the interior. The pump on the attack engine was switched to foam, and the burning engine compartment of the pickup was covered with a thin layer of foam to smother the fire. The interior was briefly foamed to make sure the fire was knocked down. Apparently, an electrical problem had caused the owner to leave his pickup at the dealership for servicing.

Seems like 2011 was the year for vehicle fires – we had three times the normal number.

We had a school bus fire, but fortunately there were no children on board. The brakes got hot, and set some oil and grease on fire.

Then, we had an engine compartment fire in a small pickup just outside of town. We were able to put the fire out quickly and minimize the damage to the engine compartment.

A few days later, a small station wagon fully loaded with household items and clothing started to smoke and burn.

After making sure the fire was out, we found a bad short in the rear brake light. Apparently, a trailer light connection had been made sometime ago, but for some reason had shorted out and set fire to the plastic bumper and back window rubber gasket. The pragmatic view held by the people who owned the car was that if it had to happen, it was best that it happened in town instead of miles from the nearest fire station. Fortunately, none of their belongings were damaged.

The worst vehicle fire that year was a burning motor home just outside of town. It was dark, about 8:30 p.m., when the pager went. The dispatcher announced there was a vehicle fire near the sawmill on highway 95. I was with the attack engine, and when we arrived, we found a motor home almost completely engulfed in fire. I started hitting the fire with the hard line, through the broken-out windshield. The wind was blowing briskly, and there were dry fields on both sides of the highway. I was worried sparks would start a field fire, so I was hosing the flying sparks in between hitting the fire inside the motor home. Something exploded, and I got hit with small debris that luckily just bounced off my heavy turnout coat and face shield.

Moving around to the passenger side of the motor home with the attack hose, I was trying to get a better angle getting the water onto the main fire. Just then, the foam line off Engine 2 went into attack, and I got hit with a blast of foam. So, I backed out and handed the hose to another firefighter while I cleaned off my visor. I looked as though I had just stepped out of a tub filled with bubble bath. We put foam through the second attack line also, and with both lines going, the foam quickly knocked down the fire.

We had barely gotten the engines back into the fire station and refilled when the pager went off again, for another vehicle fire. This one was a fifth-wheel trailer that had caught fire while parked in the owner's driveway. Fortunately, the owners saw something glowing in the trailer and called the fire department. We knocked down the fire quickly, and during mop-up, found where some bedding had been pushed up against a light that was accidentally left on. The bedding had smoldered until it finally burst into flame and started melting the plastic curtains and wall covering. If the owners hadn't seen the glowing fire when they did, this fire would have been much worse, and would have threatened to extend into the nearby garage and house.

Long 2012 Season

The morning briefing completed, Salmon River's water tender and two engines headed to their assignment - back up John Day Creek for structure protection. There was a possibility of burning out some unburned sections of the hills, so the incident management team wanted additional protection in the area should this happen. We all arrived at the main ranch house up John Day Creek, our staging area, where we engaged with the division and structure operations superintendents discussing the day's plans. The hillside to the west had burned yesterday, but there was a lot of unburned fuel on the east side of the canyon. We set up at the same junction as the day before, then worked on mopping up the burned hillside. The fire in John Day Creek had calmed down, so our job was simply to put out smokes and be prepared to roll to if requested for structure protection elsewhere.

There was concern over missing cows scattered in the area, especially since the landowner's son had found two burned cows already that morning, and feared for some fifty more that were still missing. And, more bad news was added; another structure had been destroyed beside the outbuilding at Twilegar subdivision.

An old mine site above the subdivision had a couple of buildings, with one of them fixed up and used as a home. It had burned to the ground, as there was no way an engine could safely get to the place and defend it. On the bright side, that was the only home lost so far

Late in the afternoon, we were released and told to stand by in case the fire team needed us for structure protection in a different area. By now, enough engines had arrived from places all over the U.S. that we were no longer needed.

Two weeks later, the fire was still burning. However, after a couple of serious growth spurts, the cooler temperatures and shorter days slowed the 48,000-acre fire down to a crawl. While catching up on my computer repair work, I was thinking of the first big fire of the season just about a month before the Sheep Fire.

In 2001, four firefighters were killed in their fire shelters on a fire in a forested canyon in Washington. In John Maclean's *The Thirtymile Fire* (Holt Paperbacks, 2007), he details how a number of the 10 Standard Fire Orders and 18 Watch Out Situations were compromised during the lead-up to this tragic ending of four lives. The critical points involved in this tragedy were: the lack of a recognized incident commander (IC); poor communications; and the work-rest guidelines. Communications during a fire incident are critical, and the lack of communications has led to many injuries and fatalities. I saw changes resulting from this tragedy, and watched a good communications process at work during the first large fire of the 2012 season in the Salmon River canyon. This wildfire was just what the doctor ordered for waking up the firefighting community in our area.

Needing to head to Boise for an overnight visit with an uncle and a computer job, I left Grangeville around noon. From the top of White Bird Summit, I saw wispy white smoke in the canyon miles ahead, somewhere in the vicinity of Riggins. My pager was open, but I could not hear any radio traffic about a fire.

Some thirty-five minutes later, I arrived in Riggins and learned that a fire was threatening structures on Pollock Road. My pager was not picking up any of the fire traffic, so I had no idea where along the Pollock Road the fire was or how bad it was. I knew the area well, though, and found the fire.

I was handed the job of taking charge of the Salmon River assignment on this fire. The Forest Service had arrived just ahead of me and took over the fire, asking us to stay and protect the homes. There were seven mobile homes threatened, along with three houses and a large metal shop. Salmon River had three engines on the fire when I arrived, and the Forest Service had two. Soon, two more Federal engines and a State engine pulled in.

As the attack was coming together, I was accosted by a homeowner. He was complaining that one of the firefighters had broken a propane fitting on one of his small tanks, causing the loss of some propane. The way he said it didn't make sense, so I had him repeat the complaint. Not wanting to take time away from the more important fire fight, I quickly explained that our concern right then was the fire. Once it was safe, I would check into the complaint and see that it was resolved.

There were two dozers close to the fire. Their owners fired them up and started cutting fireline along the hillside, until it got too steep to operate. A helicopter arrived with a water bucket and dropped water onto the hard-to-reach portions of the fire. Along the top of the fire, where it was too steep for the dozers and too rocky to dig fireline quickly, a few loads of retardant were dropped by SEATs. With the fire's progress stopped, the worst was over. It was time to catch a breath and mop up.

Looking into the propane line complaint, the volunteer firefighter responsible for the breakage was a propane delivery man; he told the resident that the problem would be fixed the next day.

The SRRFD was released, but I was asked to bring in a water tender to refill the Forest Service engines. After positioning the water tender, the incident commander arrived to my location and transferred command to a trainee on the fire.

The IC was to stay nearby and offer assistance if needed, but the trainee was to take over the fire. The trainee had no problem with the arrangements, so the IC radioed the crew leaders on the fire to announce that command was being transferred. If a crew leader did not acknowledge, then the IC called again on the radio to that person and restated the command change, and asked again for acknowledgment. When they'd all acknowledged, the IC radioed dispatch and repeated the message, then the new IC got on the radio and announced that he was in charge.

A little while later, the helicopter crew radioed to ask whether there were any more tasks for them on this fire. The IC asked each crew leader if they needed helicopter work in their area. When they all said no, the IC released the helicopter. There was no doubt regarding communications on this fire.

One of the Forest Service crew bosses took pity on me and gave me an MRE (meal ready to eat) bag. We both sat down to eat. Remembering the days of the C-rats, I found the plastic bagged arrangement a challenge, but located the entrée and promptly ripped open the bag. I dug into the cold meal. I was unsure what the crew boss was waiting for, but by the time I had my entrée scarfed down, I realized that his had steam coming out of it. I hadn't ever used one of these newer style MREs and didn't know about the special heater bag. The crew boss was polite and didn't say a word, but I'll bet he is still laughing!

As dusk settled in and the fire calmed down, the Forest Service released my water tender, so I refilled and returned the tender to its station.

The fire season for Grangeville was fairly quiet, until September. Before the season-ending rains finally came, the Grangeville Rural Fire Department was put to the test. It was about 8:30 a.m. when the pager tones went off. We needed to respond to a field fire just south of town. I was visiting with the assistant chief when the call came, so he hopped in the car and we drove to the station. The chief was responding directly, and the attack engine was just getting ready to leave, so the assistant chief and I climbed aboard the second rural engine. One of our firefighters, a professional truck driver, ran into the station and asked about the water tender. It was suggested he warm it up and get it ready.

As we were heading to the fire, the chief arrived at the fire and told the attack engine to keep going – there was a second fire farther south of the first. We stopped at the first fire and attacked it. While heading to the second fire, the attack engine crew spotted a third fire. From their vantage point, it looked like a house burning. The chief ordered another engine to head our way. Since the tender was warmed up and ready, it was agreed to have it come instead.

When the attack engine got closer to the third fire, they saw that a house was not involved, but they did see a fourth fire. About this time one of our volunteers, a Forest Service employee, grabbed a Forest Service radio on his way out of the office and radioed for two Forest Service engines to respond. Both engines arrived quickly and jumped on the second fire.

The rancher who owned the property had a pump and tank on a trailer and was working over the first fire, which freed up Grangeville's Engine 2 to jump on the third fire. The water tender arrived and helped the attack engine on the fourth fire.

A couple of us were thinking arson, and figured on having law enforcement involved in the investigation. However, it was quickly determined that the fires were caused by a powerline/transformer that had blown and apparently back fed down some ground wires to set grass and shrubs on fire. Fortunately, the power blip that caused these fires did not any more fires.

In the middle of the night, we had to go back to the third fire, which had been burning in a thick hedge of junipers. Apparently, a hot ember was missed during mop-up, and it found some unburned needles and flamed up. We foamed the area, which for sure put out the juniper hedge this time. Nearly a week later, we had to go back to the first fire. Apparently, a pile of cow manure near the edge of the burned grass had smoldered and been missed, when the landowner checked over the burned area.

Even after some rain, the fire season was still hanging on.

On October 18, I was in the middle of a computer repair job when the page went out for Grangeville to respond to a grass fire east of town. Some of the firefighters didn't understand the address given over the radio and headed in the wrong direction. I arrived at the station just as the two engines left going the wrong way. So, I started the water tender and headed out of town in the right direction. Realizing their mistake, the drivers turned their engines around and headed for the fire. We all arrived just in time.

The fire had burned to within thirty feet of one house, but thanks to the work of the chief, one of the volunteers, and a neighbor, it didn't get any closer. There was a dirt road alongside the field that slowed the fire down on its way toward a house to the west. The highway was to the north, but a building sat between it and the fire. To the east was a frightened horse, a couple of homes and more grass and brush. To the south was a hill with thick brush, and on top of the hill were a couple of homes. The engines jumped into the fray, splitting up and quickly hitting the fire's perimeter.

It took a couple of hours, but the fire was contained, and the perimeter was wetted down again for good measure.

Not quite three hours later, Grangeville was called out for another field fire. This time the fire was smaller, but it was threatening one home. The air was fairly quiet, so the fire crept along instead of moving fast. There was a small tree farm about 250 feet from the fire, with tall, thick dry grass surrounding it. The engines jumped on the fire quickly and kept it to under an acre.

That little bit of rain we had apparently fooled a few people into thinking they could safely burn without having to worry about losing control of the fire.

The wildfire season still wasn't finished, as we had yet another wildfire call a few weeks later. One of the assistant chiefs and I were the first to arrive at the fire station for a call to a grass fire a few miles outside of town. Taking the attack engine, we arrived to a fast spreading grass fire heading toward a couple of large shops and a house.

The wind was brisk and cold. The assistant chief had a jacket on; I did not. So, the assistant chief jumped in the back of the attack engine, fired up the pump and operated the nozzle while I drove. The priority was to hit the east side, then hit the head. The assistant chief, operating the nozzle, quickly knocked down a path through the fire, opening a hole to where I could drive into the black. We quickly attacked the east edge, the assistant chief maneuvering the nozzle while I drove the engine at a quick pace. Engine 2 arrived, and started working along the west side. The attack engine, moving quickly, worked around the head and met up with Engine 2 on the west side, containing the fire. All that was left was to mop up, call it good, and go home.

Other than the residents having a scare for a short time, this fire was one of the fun ones! I remembered my first field fire with the Grangeville Rural Fire Department, how I thought fighting the fire from inside the engine was being lazy. Here was a prime example of where fighting the fire from the engine, in the black, was quick, effective and safe. And a heck of a lot less work!

Still Going

The busy year of 2012 finally closed, after a few chimney fires and dumpster fire calls. The year 2013 started as normal, with a few chimney fires and dumpster fire calls.

Near the end of January, we were paged to a house fire; the dispatcher said the fire was in the second-floor bedroom. One of the volunteer firefighters, who lived next door to the house, had been outside looking at the house less than thirty minutes before the page. He had not seen anything at that time.

As soon as we got the page, this same firefighter grabbed his fire extinguisher, and ran out the door headed for the house. He realized quickly that with the heavy fire boiling out the window, the extinguisher would be useless. When we arrived with the engines, the bedroom was fully involved and fire was rolling down the stairway.

The roof was steep. It was snowing, so attempting a roof ventilation was not our first choice. Two interior attack teams tried to get to the fire upstairs but were beaten back by the tremendous heat. Horizontal ventilation was not working, and we needed to cut a hole in the roof to vertically vent the heat and gasses. We almost had the fire knocked down because of the volume of water we were throwing at it, but the fire took only a short break before it ran amok again.

The walls were tongue-and-groove pine over particle board, so there was no drywall to slow the fire's progression. Until we could get inside to work the fire, it was going to keep biting us in the butt. As the fire moved forward into the opposite side of the house, it finally breached through the roof. The heat upstairs was waning, so a few of us were able to tread carefully through the upstairs and start mopping up the stubborn flames.

Six hours after the first attack, we finally were able to load the engines, return to the station, and be ready for the next call. It is always a lousy feeling to be leaving an untenable structure. We did our best, but it was not good enough.

In less than a week, we were called in the early morning for another house fire. This was a single story, with flame shooting out one end of the attic. The roof looked a little weak, but it was less steep and not snow-covered like the house the week before. One team laddered the building and started a ventilation hole, while another team started an interior attack. This fire didn't get such a big head start, so we were able to keep the damage to just three rooms and part of the attic.

May arrived, and the temperatures jumped up quickly. Areas were drying, and the cheat grass in the Salmon River canyon was already turning brown.

One morning, something told me to throw in my wildland gear bag as I headed to Riggins for a day of computer repair jobs. While working on a computer at my wife's family's house, I walked to the car for my tools. I smelled smoke. My sister-in-law saw the flames at the same time. I radioed dispatch to tone out the Salmon River Rural Fire Department for a wildfire, and gave the location.

My brother-in-law saw a second fire along the highway. As he headed to that fire with a shovel, I headed to the first fire. I radioed dispatch that we now had two fires, and to notify the Forest Service. As I arrived at the first fire, I saw a third fire. I radioed dispatch again, suggesting that a vehicle heading south must be dragging something to be starting these fires. Dispatch toned out Riggins Fire Department to assist. SRRFD Engine 3 arrived and stopped the forward spread of the third fire.

The first fire was moving uphill, trying to hook around a rock slide to get to some houses. A couple of local people had hoses out and were watching for spot fires. The Riggins fire chief arrived, so I sent him up the highway to the second fire. He noticed yet another fire. So, he called for his second engine to help. The Forest Service started arriving, and jumped on three more growing fires.

It turns out that dragging chains from a towed boat trailer had started eight fires along a four mile stretch of U.S. Highway 95, threatening five homes and burning about thirty acres.

Fortunately, the Forest Service arrived in force, especially for this time of year, before their summer fire crews are on board. Both the Nezperce and Payette National Forests sent numerous engines, and the Payette even re-assigned a smokejumper training session to the fire, allowing eight smokejumpers to jump the top of the largest of the fires.

The next morning, the Grangeville Rural Fire Department was paged out at about 4 a.m. to a barn fire. Unfortunately, the barn was actually a large machine shop just finished being remodeled. This fire was about three miles from the nearest water supply, so we set up the 3000 gallon snap tank and portable pump. We shuttled water using the water tender, keeping the primary engine pumping water to the fire. This was the first time we had used the tank and pump system on an actual fire operation.

The look on the faces of the young owners said it all, reinforcing my dislike of structure fires. Their livelihood, burnt. If someone had seen the fire twenty minutes earlier, we may have had a chance to save part of the business, instead of mopping up a completely destroyed building.

A month later, Grangeville Rural was paged out at 1:15 a.m. for a vehicle crash, the vehicle was on fire. As we are responding to the scene, the dispatcher relayed the message that the vehicle was fully involved, no one made it out. *Ah shit, damn it.*

If this call had been during the day, I would have thought it to be an EMT disaster drill. They have these drills every couple of years. But, in the middle of the night, this would not be a drill. If anyone was still half asleep, that radio transmission just woke them up.

Upon arrival, we started foaming the burning vehicle, trying to get the fire knocked down. Fortunately the vehicle, a pickup, was upright and just 20 feet off the road. It had been stopped by trees, otherwise it could have rolled down the steep hillside. A broken tree was laying across the cab and engine compartment of the vehicle, while the bed of the pickup was laying in the trees about 25 feet away. The fire was quickly knocked down by the foam.

With the arrival of the EMTs, a search was started for the occupants. Three teenagers were found. We couldn't touch a thing. There was nothing to be done until the investigators did their job. While waiting for the investigators, three of us volunteered to stay with the attack engine in case of a flare up. Everyone else was released to go home. The State Police brought in experts to reconstruct the accident, while the coroner made arrangements for handling the victims. By the time we made it back home it was nearly time to start a typical day. But, there was nothing typical about the day.

While we wait for the next fire call, life marches on. There is talk about a very busy wildfire season in the west, including our area. We worry a little about the politics governing the agencies handling wildfires in our area, wondering how federal and state budget cuts will affect our ability to deal with wildfire. As John N. Maclean wrote in his book *Fire and Ashes: On the Front Lines of American Wildfire* (Henry Holt and Company, 2003):

"The emphasis on safety in recent decades has saved lives. But the simplest lesson of fighting fire may have become a casualty: if you are going to put out a fire, hit it aggressively while it is small."

With looming budget cuts, the "big unknown" is how quick and aggressive the agencies can be with fewer personnel and equipment available. How will that affect our ability to deal with another Blackerby or Poe Cabin fire scenario in which multiple structures are threatened by wildfire? In the meantime, we continue to train and prepare for whatever we get called to - and hope to avoid tragedies.

One of these days, the time will come to turn in my fire

gear and leave the firefighting to the younger ones. Until then, my radio is on my belt or by my bed, and my fire gear bags are in the car, waiting for me to go kick some ash. And, when the page tone goes off, the adrenaline still flows and the questions are still asked: what's burning, how badly, who's going to be there to lead and to help, where's the water, is anyone inside?

ACKNOWLEDGEMENTS

Remembering the good ole days, thanks goes to crew superintendents Wally Acton and John Maupin. They kept us alive, but kicked our butts doing it. To Gene Pennington, for training us volunteers to safely work more like professional firefighters, and less like 'keystone cops.' Certainly, thanks go to the volunteers of both the Salmon River Rural and Grangeville Fire Departments. They have my back, while I have theirs.

Special thanks go to John Maclean, famous author of numerous books on wildland fires, for putting me in contact with Kelly Andersson. Kelly provided the stimulus, edited the manuscript, assisted in the design of the front cover, set up the format of the text, and provided helpful suggestions.

Numerous people provided photographs for me to use, but unfortunately I had to grab just a few. Thanks go to David Rauzi, Idaho County Free Press, for providing the cover photographs, and photographs 6, 10, 12, 13, 15, 16, 19, 20, 21 and 23; to Rick Lance for photograph 14; to Lona Travis for photograph 8; to Dorothy and Butch Walker for photograph 5, and to Margo Russell Bambacigno for the author photograph.

A very special appreciation goes to my wife, Cindy, and our two children, Dominic and Carmen. Cindy did the final editing, proving to me that I do not know the difference between prepositions and verbs, or where to put commas!

ABOUT THE AUTHOR

John lives in Grangeville, Idaho, with Cindy, his wife of 38 years. They have two children and two grandchildren. He can be reached at pcrcs136@gmail.com.

www.ingramcontent.com/pod-product-compliance
Lightning Source LLC
Chambersburg PA
CBHW071701090426
42738CB00009B/1612